4·50

INSHORE BOAT ANGLING

INSHORE BOAT ANGLING

A PRACTICAL GUIDE

RUSSELL SYMONS

WARD LOCK

DEDICATION

This book is dedicated to my wife Pat and my daughter Karen, without whose help and forebearance it would never have been written. To say thank you to all of the many people who have helped and inspired me over the years seems somehow inadequate, but I say thank you anyway, especially to Jim Randall who read the manuscript and pulled me up on a few things, to Spencer Vibart who taught me about dedication and values; to Melvin Russ, Editor of *Sea Angler* who still insults me when a deadline is near, and to my late friend Colin Gibbs, whose friendship and photographic expertise is a never-ending source of inspiration.

A Cassell imprint

© Russell Symons 1991

First published 1991 by Ward Lock
Villiers House, 41/47 Strand, London WC2N 5JE

British Library Cataloguing in Publication Data
Symons, Russell
Inshore boat angling: a practical guide.
1. Sea angling
I. Title
799.16
ISBN 0–7063–6982–3

Printed and bound in Great Britain by Courier Int., Tiptree, Essex

Photography by Russell Symons

CONTENTS

Jim Randell in his boat Marlin, *a Tamar 2000 displacement-hulled, diesel-engined vessel. Jim had* Marlin *fitted out with a full complement of electronics and everything else that the serious angler could wish for. With Jim's lifetime of experience in West country waters, the* Marlin *and he made a formidable team.*

FOREWORD

You could say that boat angler Russ Symons has saltwater running through his veins. A man who has spent his life angling from big charter boats and small inshore dinghies, what he doesn't know about handling a boat, fishing from a boat, tackle, baits and techniques isn't worth knowing.

Actually, Russ comes from a nautical background. Born and bred in the great naval city of Plymouth, his dad was a navy man, and Russ continued very much in the tradition by working in the Devonport Naval dockyard where he taught apprentices engineering. And it is this engineering background, which demands attention to detail, that has made Russ a great angler. For when he gets his teeth into something, he wants to know how everything works right down to the last nut and bolt, keel band, engine spark plug and hook.

Always a great believer in giving the fish some sort of fighting chance, he is an outstanding advocate of fishing with balanced tackle. In fact, he holds at least one IGFA world class line record, and at one time held the British boat-caught conger eel record . . . even if it was only for a couple of days.

Boat angling demands a high degree of skill to be effective, and in this book Russ has amassed everything he has learned the hard way, to help you become a better boat angler. His advice is always sound and worthy of note. His views on safety, navigation and seamanship run parallel with mine and whether you are fishing from a large or small boat Russ's advice should be followed. Foolish men should never put to sea in boats.

Having known and fished with Russ over some 15 years I have become used to his dry sense of humour. I trust that you enjoy this book, and his personal anecdotes, as I have enjoyed his company over all those years.

Mel Russ, Editor
Sea Angler
Boat Angler and
Sea Angling magazines

CHAPTER ONE

THE ANGLER'S BOAT

It is not difficult to see why the number of anglers purchasing their own boat continues to increase, and why the small boat angler becomes so totally engrossed in his role as shipwright/mechanic/seaman/skipper and finally – almost as an afterthought – angler.

The shorebound angler has to be able to cast, dig bait and figure out where the fish are, or maybe he sits hopefully on the shingle, just waiting for a fish to find his bait. The small boat angler's approach is different: not only does he have to work harder, trailing and launching his boat, he often has a different, more vital attitude – almost as if he has said to himself, 'After all this trouble, I am going to find some fish.' The fact that he may well put them back to grow a bit bigger is irrelevant.

In my experience the small boat angler is on the one hand the most dedicated angler and on the other the most independent, difficult-to-please character. Perhaps this is not difficult to understand when we realize that in a small boat there is little room for silly mistakes, errors of judgement, ignorance or temper. The sea has no favourites and only right and proper practice is good enough when you are out in a boat.

We who take to sea in small boats are among the most vulnerable of any group of sportsmen, putting our own lives and those of our crew at risk every time. So what we look for in a small boat is somewhat different from what is offered by the pleasure craft that many of our boat designers assume will suit anglers. Hardier anglers are content with the basic open boat, and there is a lot to be said for the accessibility,

all-round vision and fish-playing room in such a boat. Indeed, in the southern USA some of the speedy, sophisticated fishing machines with a central console are no more than open boats.

Our climate, however, calls for a craft that has some shelter even if it is minimal, such as the forward 'dodger' found on the traditional Cornish crab boat. This gives shelter from the wind and rain without taking up too much of the open deck space favoured by experienced anglers. What is of consequence is the shape of the hull, which will be either 'conventional displacement', 'semi-displacement' or at the out-and-out 'planing' type. The difference between these is explained on page 10.

When choosing a boat you can spend many hours pondering the pros and cons of fibreglass versus wood, of fast versus slow, of the economies of inboard and outboard engines, and so on. But the perfect boat does not exist. A boat that is good for one thing is not so good for another, and so every boat is a compromise. The experienced boat owner will already have a fund of experience on which he can base his decisions. Personal preferences count for a lot when buying a boat and, balancing these against hard-won experience, the experienced boat owner will often know just by looking at it that a particular hull shape and size is potentially right for what he wants. This sort of experience does not come easily and too often follows expensive mistakes.

When you are buying your first boat, look hard, listen hard and say nothing, it is so easy to look at a hull in a showroom or at a dock and be taken in by the excitement of ownership and the salesman's smooth patter. Never buy a boat until you have had a second opinion, a proper ride in it and have slept on the decision.

What size and shape of boat might suit your needs best? You are probably already a reasonably experienced angler, because nobody buys a boat and takes up fishing at the same time! You are likely to have a good idea of where you want to go, how far offshore, what sort of sea conditions might be encountered, what depth of water you will be working in and so on.

Do you want the boat to be trailable? If so, too big a boat will hinder rather than help. On the other hand, if you want to go further offshore than is prudent in a small dinghy, you will need something in the 20–30 ft (6–9 m) class which can take the sort of seas you are more likely to encounter offshore. This sort of boat will usually offer more creature comforts: bunks, a head (toilet), a gas cooker and so on. It is also likely that in a boat of this size you will have an inboard engine, perhaps a diesel. You will probably have a permanent mooring rather than using a trailer or leaving it in a boat park, as you would with a small boat.

Choosing and buying an angling boat requires more than just casual thought. It demands careful consideration in which every variable is weighed against your needs and what you can afford. Buy in haste and repent at leisure, to adapt the saying about marriage.

Orkney Coastliner, a super little boat ideally suited to estuary and close inshore angling. It pops on and off a trailer like a dream and achieves a surprising turn of speed with just a 20 hp outboard engine.

HULL SHAPE

There are three basic types of hull which concern the angler: the traditional displacement hull, the more modern planing hull and a hybrid of the two known as the semi-displacement hull.

The displacement hull

This type of hull displaces water as it passes through it giving a slower, more sympathetic ride, and so is a more 'kindly' boat when conditions are rough. Most of the traditional wooden-hulled boats are of this design. For example, the traditional Cornish 'crabber' was specifically designed to be low and heavy in the water, so that it could cope with the huge waves which roll across the Atlantic and sweep up the Western Approaches. These heavy wooden boats had their hull shapes refined by generations of Cornish shipwrights, ultimately to become the classic displacement hull for a boat of under 50 ft (15 m). This shape can cope with bad weather and provides a good platform onto which to haul the crab pots. No better hull shape has ever evolved for an angling boat.

The displacement hull has been copied and reproduced in fibreglass and although, in the opinion of many, these boats do not 'sit' as well in the water as did the wooden boats, they are remarkably good.

The displacement hull is slower than the planing hull; its maximum speed is proportionate to its waterline length. The power required to push it through the water to this maximum speed, however, is considerably less than that of the heavy-duty power units required by a planing hull.

Displacement hulls are to be found all over the world and they make for a roomy, comfortable and safe angling boat.

The planing hull

The planing hull is a comparatively modern concept in angling boat design, and its evolution into the superb hull shapes available today owes much to American influence. This type of hull does not push through the water like the displacement hull, but 'planes' over the top at a much faster maximum speed. Its disadvantage is that it is not such a comfortable ride in rough conditions.

The semi-displacement hull

A semi-displacement hull is a hybrid of the traditional displacement hull and the more modern planing hull, which, so theory has it, will get up 'on the plane' for speed and sit in the water like a displacement hull when at rest. This would seem to be a perfect compromise for an angling boat, but unfortunately some of these hulls, instead of offering all the advantages of both types of boat, seem to incorporate most if not all of their drawbacks.

There are some excellent semi-displacement hulls around and some which are really awful, so if you are considering a hull of this type, make sure you give it an extended sea trial, particularly in sloppy conditions.

Fibreglass versus wooden hulls

There are valid arguments for wooden boats as opposed to low-maintenance GRP (Glass-reinforced Plastic) hulled boats. But on balance, unless you have the time and inclination to devote yourself to the care of a wooden boat, GRP is a more practical material, particularly if you are the average family man with a house and car to maintain as well.

Planked wood boats are generally heavier than GRP boats and are not so easy to take in and out of the water or to trail behind a car. Often a small wooden boat will have an inboard engine and can be found on a mooring. You may well ask why some anglers prefer a wooden hull with all its potential headaches.

Apart from the aesthetic appeal and reassuring feel of wood, many bass anglers believe that the combination of wood boat and inboard engine is better for whiffing/trolling for bass and pollack. Also, the engine exhaust goes into the atmosphere and not into the water that your lures have to swim through. A further advan-

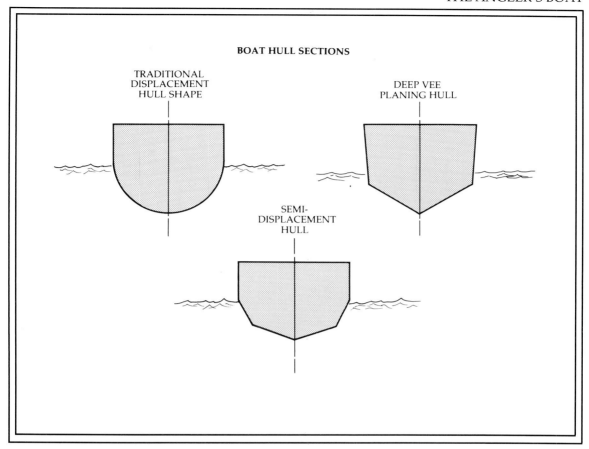

BOAT HULL SECTIONS

TRADITIONAL DISPLACEMENT HULL SHAPE

DEEP VEE PLANING HULL

SEMI-DISPLACEMENT HULL

tage is that wood deadens the engine and noises made by the angler. 'Get yourself a wood boat if you want to catch fish' is the view held by many experienced anglers and 'plastic boats with an egg whisk on the back are noisy, too light, and put a stink into the water' is a hard argument to refute when the results over many seasons often bear out this advice.

Nevertheless, many of the modern GRP designs are remarkably good, and if the sea begins to get sloppy, the fast planing hull can get you home quickly, before the weather deteriorates sufficiently to test the boat's performance. After all, as the planing hull advocates often say, 'Angling is for pleasure, not punishment' – and they are right! Furthermore, when on the drift or at anchor the planing hull has a quicker, less predictable motion in the water than the tradi-

tional round-bilged displacement hull.

The Americans prefer angling boats with the deep vee type of planing hull, whereas in Europe the 'cathedral' or tri-hull shape with its rectangular deck shape has gained much favour. The British Dell Quay Dory and American Boston Whaler make superb fishing platforms, and there is probably more usable space on a 17-ft (5 m) dory than on a 21-ft (6·5 m) boat with a conventionally shaped hull.

Fibreglass boats cost less than new wooden boats, and are much easier to keep clean and generally maintain, since repairs can be made by anglers with no more than moderate DIY skills. Materials and specific advice on repairs are freely available from GRP merchandisers such as Strand Glass, who have depots all over the country.

The 22-ft Seaworker is a fast, seaworthy angling vessel, which many inshore boat anglers consider to be the height of their aspirations: big enough to go wrecking, yet small enough to work the close inshore marks.

GRP MAINTENANCE

It is a mistake to assume that GRP boats need no maintenance at all, since the high-gloss gel coat on the outside needs regular inspection and repair. Minor bumps and bangs against a floating object or a dock wall will chip or scratch the gel coat, leaving it vulnerable to penetration by salt water, which in turn can lead to osmosis, the salt water soaking into the fibreglass causing the hull to bubble and delaminate – a serious problem.

Inspect the hull thoroughly at least once each season and repair or fill any minor damage to the gel coat with gel of the same colour. Small packs of gel coat can be purchased for this purpose. Mix the ingredients in the pack to the proportion and colour as directed in the instructions. Scrape and sand the damage so that it is thoroughly clean, then carefully wipe it clean with a rag impregnated sparingly with acetone, before filling the scratch or gouge with the gel. Then cover the spot with clear adhesive tape to exclude the air and leave undisturbed for 24 hours. After peeling away the tape, blend in the patch with wet and dry abrasive paper and lots of water.

At least once a year clean the hull thoroughly with fibreglass cleaning compound, removing any tar spots or other marks. Then give the hull a good coat of wax polish, since not only does this improve the look of the hull but protects it as well.

If your boat is kept on a mooring give the underside of the hull a periodic paint with an anti-fouling preparation to prevent any marine weed growth as this can slow your boat considerably and increase your fuel bills enormously.

ENGINES

The larger planing-hulled angling boats might have an inboard diesel engine driving a 'stern-drive' unit, but most angling planing hulls used in Britain are under 20 ft (6 m) and powered by one or more outboard engines. The typical privately owned larger displacement boat is 20–27 ft (6–8 m) long and powered by a diesel engine of 20–70 hp which, if adequately maintained, will deliver excellent economy and reliability, pushing the boat along at a steady 7–10 knots.

Inboard diesel engines

When an engine gives a cough, stops and all falls quiet, the feeling of dread is almost tangible. The boat is helpless, and fiddling about trying to get an engine going again in a sloppy sea with the smell of a hot engine and fuel pervading everything is not an experience which can be recommended.

Proper maintenance must never be neglected, and if you have the skills to do it yourself, do not skip it just because you would rather be out fishing. If you cannot do it yourself, have the engine maintained regularly by a competent engineer.

The modern diesel engine is very reliable and given care and a supply of clean fuel will often go for years without major problems. But neglect is the forerunner of trouble and adhering to a proper basic maintenance routine as detailed in the owner's manual will often be enough to ensure reliable performance, for it is reliability which the angler requires above all else.

The worst enemy of the diesel engine is contaminated fuel. When carrying fuel, make sure the containers are clean and tightly stoppered, and use a clean funnel when filling the tank. Make sure the fuel-line filters are changed at regular intervals and that a water separator is also included in the fuel line – you cannot be too fussy with diesel fuel.

It is obviously best to keep diesel tanks topped up, but if you are forgetful and run out of fuel you will have to bleed air from the engine before it will run again. This procedure will be detailed in the owner's manual. Do not wait until you are at sea to learn how to bleed an engine. Learn the procedure while you are moored up quietly one day, or maybe even get your mechanic or a knowledgeable friend to give you some instruction.

Nearly all diesel engines today are water-cooled by means of a closed-circuit freshwater system, which is itself cooled by sea water being pumped through a heat exchanger. It is important to keep an eye on the temperature gauge. Overheating is also indicated if the engine begins to run roughly and steam is emitted from the sea-water discharge. The most likely reason is a blockage in the sea-water inlet, usually plastic bags or seaweed. After stopping the engine, close the seacock next to the sea-water inlet and clear the blockage. Do not forget to top up the freshwater header tank.

Oil changes and greasing are comparatively simply DIY maintenance tasks. The simplest and one of the most important tasks is greasing the stern tube bearing. This is usually accomplished by means of a 'screw-down' greasing unit on top of the stern tube unit. Make sure you use only the grease recommended by the makers and keep the grease reservoir topped up. Each trip screw the top down a turn or so, so that fresh grease is forced down around the propeller shaft. Oil becomes 'tired' after prolonged use: its lubricating properties become less effective and the additives which are so essential in a marine engine stop working.

The inside of a marine engine is far more prone to condensation than a car engine. It may be used only once or twice a week, and maybe at even longer intervals if the weather is bad for a prolonged period. The water produced by this condensation combines with the residue of engine combustion and forms acids which attack the engine's innards. Additives found in modern marine engine oil neutralize these acids and prevent the condensate from forming rust, so it is wise to change your oils in accordance with the engine manufacturer's recommendations.

Change the oil filter regularly. In marine engines the oil filter is usually situated in an easily accessible position to encourage you to change it after the running time recommended by the maker has elapsed.

Outboard engines

Outboard engines today have come a long way from the cantankerous contraptions they once were. Reliability and a high power-to-weight ratio is the aim of every manufacturer and a measure of these engines' success is the number that can be seen hanging from the sterns of a high proportion of small inshore angling boats. Anglers are perhaps the sternest critics of an outboard's performance. We are not concerned as much with the look of an engine as with whether it starts first pull on the starter cord or jab on the electric start button.

Most outboards are two-stroke engines although a few manufacturers are now introducing a four-stroke engine particularly in the 10–15 hp range. The development of the latter is almost entirely due to the demand of American anglers who wanted an engine which would run all day at low revs without the plugs oiling up, as will most two-strokes. With 60 million American anglers the market was certainly large enough to justify the development of these engines.

A four-stroke engine is quieter and more economical in its performance than an equivalent two-stroke; its disadvantage is that it costs more to buy. Two-stroke engines as well as being cheaper to buy than four-strokes are more than adequate for the angling requirements of British anglers, who rarely require the prolonged low-speed trolling speeds so often used in more exotic climates.

When choosing an outboard it pays to check what other small boat owners are using and to evaluate how much power is required to give the optimum performance for your boat. As well as asking the dealer, talk to other boat owners, since their advice and views are invaluable. It is a mistake to overpower a boat, just as it is a mistake to underpower with an engine which will have to be run flat out to give you the power required by your hull.

For a 15–17-ft (4·5–5 m) displacement-hull fishing dinghy, which may have to carry two or three anglers and a lot of tackle against the fast currents which are common in the best fishing spots, an engine of 7.5–15 hp seems to have evolved as the best compromise between cost and performance. A planing hull of the same length will require engines of 20 hp and upwards to give optimum performance. For larger planing hulls there is a choice between one large outboard engine or two smaller engines. The two-engine rig is an added safety factor should one engine fail while you are fishing offshore. The one larger engine is cheaper to buy and uses less petrol. Some anglers compromise by buying a larger engine and a smaller 'get you home' engine which will not lift the boat onto the plane, yet will improve safety as well as being useful at slow speeds.

Outboard maintenance

Careful maintenance of an outboard is essential to maintain the performance and reliability of which the modern engine is capable. First and most important is the correct oil/petrol mix. Read the manufacturer's instruction book thoroughly and ensure that you understand how to obtain the 50-to-1 or other recommended proportion of oil to petrol, particularly if metric measures are used. Most manufacturers recommend a higher proportion of oil to petrol for the first 10 hours, the 'running in' period. This additional oil provides lubrication to the machined surfaces while they bed in one to the other. For the first two hours do not operate the motor at more than half throttle. After the first 10 hours it is a good idea to clean the plugs and get the timing adjusted by the nearest service agency.

It is important that a proper two-stroke oil be used in this oil/petrol mix for outboard engines. This is particularly so now that some outboard manufacturers are using a computer-controlled

Mariner 25-hp outboard engine, with its cowling removed to show the works. Check for loose nuts and bolts periodically, then spray all over with a water dispersant such as WD 40.

oil-injection system whereby the oil is not mixed in the fuel tank but is contained in a header tank in the engine compartment. This system varies the oil/petrol mix as demanded by sensors within the engine. In some instances the mix may be as low as 200-to-1, which means that at low speeds, when the engine is under little stress, the plugs are not likely to oil up. Since less oil is being used, the necessity to use the right oil is more important than ever before. To think you can save a few pennies by using any old oil in place of the specially formulated two-stroke oils is to invite long-term trouble and a substantial reduction in your engine's life. Today's special two-stroke oils contain hi-tech ingredients to ensure that the engine burns without depositing the highly abrasive ash that is the by-product of some oils on combustion. Another constituent is a type of lubricant which will lubricate piston and cylinder walls at the higher two-stroke temperatures without 'burning off'. In short, save yourself trouble by using only a reputable two-stroke oil.

Petrol/oil ratio for outboard engines

Petrol/oil	Petrol (litres)				
	5	10	15	20	25
	Oil (millilitres)				
25–1	200	400	600	800	1000
50–1	100	200	300	400	500
100–1	50	100	150	200	250

With a small outboard that you detach and take home after use, always carry the engine powerhead upward, otherwise water will get back into the cylinders and elsewhere, causing all sorts of internal problems. After using the engine always try to flush through with fresh water to clean the salt water from inside the cooling system. There are two methods of doing this. Mariner engines have a screw-in hosepipe connector so that your garden hose can be used to flush the system with the engine running at low revs, while other makes usually have an accessory to allow a similar procedure.

The other method is to run the engine in a large container of fresh water. A 45-gallon (200l) oil drum with one end removed and a metal or wooden plinth bolted to it simulating the transom pad of the boat is the favourite of engine mechanics. The oil drum is filled with fresh water and the engine clamped to the plinth with its leg submerged so that the cooling inlets draw from and discharge the water back into the tank. Often the water looks most unattractive with a heavy film of oil on top, but this is deliberate: the oil is drawn up inside the cooling galleries, leaving a film which will further protect the aluminium.

This simple procedure is well worth the effort, since it improves engine life and reliability. After it has been flushed through, the outside of the engine should be washed down with fresh water and then sprayed with WD-40 or a similar water-dispersant oil to protect its outward appearance. Then remove the engine cowl and give the whole engine a spray with the WD-40, particularly the electrical parts and the ignition system. This only takes a minute, but ensures that you will not have any of the problems that damp might cause.

At the same time inspect for any deterioration or damage. Check your propeller for nicks or damage, and lightly dress any minor damage with a file. Anything other than minor damage, such as cracks, distortion or a big chunk knocked off a blade can result in the propeller running out of balance, which can soon knock out bearings and gears. Provided the damage is not terminal there are firms advertised in the yachting magazines which can repair propellers for a reasonable sum.

Depending on how frequently the engine is used the lower-unit gearbox oil should be changed at regular intervals. Never make the mistake of trying to pinch a few pennies by using oil other than that recommended by the engine's manufacturer for this purpose. The gears in this gearbox are of a design which demands a heavy-duty extreme-pressure (EP) oil and use of anything other than this type of oil will quickly result in an expensive repair bill or, even worse, problems at sea.

The procedure for replenishing this oil is not difficult. Using a large screwdriver which will fit the vent and filler screw heads properly, remove the filler screw and fibre washer, then the vent screw and washer, putting them both in a safe but handy position. Allow a few minutes for the used oil to drain from the gear box. Place the nozzle of the tube of new oil into the filler hole and squeeze the tube until the oil starts to flow out of the vent screw hole. Holding the tube in position, screw the vent screw and washer back finger-tight, and be ready with the filler screw. Remove the neck of the oil tube from the filler screw hole and quickly replace the filler screw. Tighten both screws to their original tightness with the screwdriver.

Occasionally apply grease where required as specified in the owner's manual, using a water-resistant marine-grade grease. Maintenance such as this pays real dividends in engine reliability and long life.

When you go afloat, always carry a spare set of plugs, correctly gapped and ready for use, a can of WD-40 and a spare pull cord. Most often when an engine gives trouble, changing the plugs and spraying the ignition system with WD-40 will effect a miraculous cure.

Winterizing your outboard

When the winter gales and cold keep the small boat angler ashore for weeks, sometimes months, the inside of an engine can deteriorate so much that it seizes up. It pays to preserve your engine when it becomes evident that the bad weather has set in. If the weather improves the engine can easily and quickly be recommissioned. It is not unusual for my engine to be preserved two or three times each winter.

The procedure is not difficult and takes perhaps 15 minutes. When you are satisfied

Remove the spark plugs regularly, and clean vigorously with a wire brush to remove any caked-on carbon deposits. Then reset the gap using the correct feeler gauge. Keep a spare set of plugs, cleaned, reset and ready to use aboard your boat.

that your engine has been thoroughly flushed through, remove the fuel line and let the engine run for a little while to use up most of the fuel in the carburettor. Then, using an aerosol can of preservative oil, spray the preservative oil into the carburettor's air intake until the engine stalls. On most engines a small plastic shroud or air-box cover will have to be removed to gain access to the air intake; this is generally retained by one or two screws.

Remove the plug leads by simply pulling them straight off the plug. Then, using a plug spanner, unscrew and remove the spark plugs. Spray preservative into the spark plug holes and then gently pull the engine over a few times. This helps to spread the lubricant around its innards, and then give the plug holes another spray to make sure.

Examine the spark plugs thoroughly and then clean them with a wire brush and reset the gap as described in the owner's manual. If you have the slightest doubt about the plugs, do not hesitate to replace them with new plugs. Check your spare set at the same time, and it is a good idea to rotate the sets of plugs throughout the season so that you are sure both sets are fully functional. When installing plugs, start with finger pressure only, to minimize the risk of cross-threading. Seat the plug snugly with a plug socket, and then just a quarter of a turn is enough to tighten it. Make sure each plug has its copper washer in place on the thread. Finally, push the plug lead firmly onto its correct plug. (Mark the leads with a felt-tip pen or adhesive tape beforehand if, like me, you tend to be forgetful.)

Most modern engines have a fuel-line filter, which can be found close to the carburettor. Generally it is simply a matter of unclipping to remove it and washing the filter element in petrol, visually inspecting it before replacement. If this filter has a renewable element, replace the element if it has had reasonable use, whether you think it needs it or not.

If the engine has points and a condenser I would renew them whether they need replacing or not, following the instructions found in the engine's handbook. If you are in doubt about doing this, either get a competent mechanic to show you or ask your dealer to replace them and tune your engine. The more modern capacitor discharge (CD) ignition systems are the ultimate in reliability and if it is working well, leave it alone!

Clean all the grease nipples and apply marine grease with a reliable grease-gun until surplus grease shows. At the same time grease all linkages, screws and clamps, checking their condition and tightness as you go.

Remove the propeller's split pin and nut. Often the prop has to be wedged with a piece of wood between a blade and the bottom of the cavitation plate in order to get the leverage necessary to undo the propeller retaining nut. Once the nut has been removed the propeller can be slid off its splined shaft. At this point the propeller can be cleaned and visually examined for damage, cracks, chunks chipped off etc., which can cause the prop to run out of balance and will in turn ruin bearings, transmission and so on.

Propellers can be repaired by specialist firms, but if the damage is bad, you will save money in the long term by buying a new one. To replace the propeller, wipe the splined shaft clean and then smear it with marine grease. Clean the inside of the propeller by pulling a rag through once or twice. Examine it for burrs or damage and when satisfied put some grease inside, working it into the splines with a finger. Slide the propeller back onto the shaft.

Grease the thread and replace the retaining nut, tightening until the original castellation lines up with the hole through the shaft, then pass the locking split pin through and bend its halves over so it cannot possibly work loose. Make sure when replacing the propeller that any thrust washers are replaced in the exact order in which they were removed.

This is a good time to replace the lower-unit lubricant as described on page 16. Do not forget to renew the fibre washers behind the vent and filler screws – they only cost pennies.

Lastly, inspect the fuel tank, fuel line and priming bulb. Visually examine the fuel line and bulb and if the rubber is starting to crack replace as necessary. Do not try to cut out the old bits and do a makeshift repair. It is not worth it, because you can be sure that if it is going to go wrong it will happen at the most awkward time.

Empty the fuel tank and remove the fuel pickup filter (generally this is a casting retained by four screws). A great deal of dirt will have collected in the bottom of the tank after even one season's use. Put some clean petrol or paraffin in the tank and slosh it around, repeating this several times until the inside of the tank seems to be free from foreign matter. Wash the fuel pickup filter until it is clean, spray the inside of the tank with preservative, then screw the fuel pickup filter and casting back into place, ensuring that the sealing gasket is in good condition. Swill the tank out with half a pint of petrol before refilling to start the next season.

At least once each season remove the outboard's propeller. Put a piece of 2 × 2-in wood between the cavitation plate and the propeller to lock the propeller against the force applied in loosening the nut.

Troubleshooting checklist

	Check	Try
ENGINE WILL NOT START	Fuel in tank	Fill with fresh petrol and use petrol conditioner to aid easy starting. Pull engine over slowly a few times after pumping fuel up with fuel-line priming bulb.
	Fuel filter clogged	Wash filter clean, or renew replaceable element.
	Engine flooded	Push choke in, pull engine over several times slowly – pull choke out, pull cord vigorously.
	Cold start	Pull choke right out.
	Electrical connections damaged or decrepit.	Check all connections, grease with Vaseline. Replace connectors and broken or worn wiring.
	Spark plugs	Remove, replace with spare set. Connections should be clean and secure and plugs of right size and type.
	Vent on petrol tank	Open to full extent.
ENGINE MISSES AT IDLING SPEEDS	Spark plugs oiled	Check petrol/oil mixture is correct. Run engine hard for a few minutes. Clean, service or replace plugs.
ENGINE MISSES AT SLOW (TROLLING) SPEEDS	Fuel supply	Check for kinked or pinched fuel line.
	Contaminated or stale petrol	Refill tank with fresh petrol/oil and use petrol conditioner.
	Throttle Electrical components defective	Reset according to manual. Ask dealer to repair.

ENGINE MISSES AT HIGH RUNNING SPEEDS	Plugs	Plugs breaking down under heavy use. Replace plugs.
	Petrol/oil mixture	Mix up new batch fresh petrol/two-stroke oil.
	Electrical connections	Tighten all loose connections. Renew damaged wiring.
	Carburettor mixture out of tune Timing out	Follow instructions in owner's manual or get dealer to tune up.
	Engine overheating	Check water intakes for blockage. Water pump failure: check 'tell-tale' water jet.
GETTING NOWHERE FAST	Propeller	Propeller must be of correct diameter and pitch for engine. Propeller hub could be slipping, or the shear pin broken. Repair or replace as necessary.
	Boat wrongly loaded	Propeller too near surface not driving. Redistribute load.
	Tilt angle incorrect	Adjust tilt angle to get boat's attitude correct.
VIBRATION	Propeller	Check propeller has not lost a blade.

Outboard Troubleshooting

'If in doubt, don't go out.' Even if you just suspect that your engine is going to let you down, get it sorted out so that you are 100 per cent confident when you do eventually put to sea. Sometimes the malfunctions are minor, but when you are in a hurry to fish you can easily overlook the obvious.

These are basic diagnostic signs which, combined with commonsense interpretation, should point you towards the fault. However, if you feel that you cannot cope with the repair, get it done professionally – the sea has no favourites.

Engine and Boat Trim

Outboard engines come as standard in two 'leg lengths', 20 in (508 mm) or long shaft, and 15 in (375 mm) or short shaft. Which is correct for your boat is determined by the transom height of your hull. The engine's cavitation plate should be about level with the keel of the boat, so this is the deciding factor in your choice of leg length when purchasing an engine.

The purpose of the cavitation plate is to prevent air from being drawn down onto the propeller, which considerably reduces its efficiency. Often in small boats the trim can be adversely effected by where you stand, so stand in the stern when you get under way and move forward only as you pick up speed. This will keep the cavitation plate functional and, even more important, keep the cooling water intakes submerged.

For maximum efficiency when the boat is under way the hull should be as close to horizontal as possible. On some hulls the transom is angled, making this horizontal position more difficult to attain. The engine's attitude to the hull can be adjusted through a series of holes and a pin (tilt pin) through the engine's clamping bracket. The degree of engine tilt should be adjusted with the boat fully loaded – that is, with anchors, tackle, battery and your regular fishing crew on board.

If the engine is adjusted inward towards the stern the thrust from the propeller will tend to raise the stern. Conversely, if it is adjusted away from the stern the propeller thrust will tend to lift the boats bow, forcing the engine to push a wide expanse of the boat's bottom through the water. With a displacement hull this might give the impression of more speed, but all you are doing is wasting petrol. Adjust the speed and trim so that the bow is cutting the water, not the bottom.

With larger engines and planing hulls this trim is critical and the engine itself may well have hydraulic trimming so that the boat's trim can be infinitely adjusted while under way to compensate for variations in sea conditions and load. Trim tabs are a further aid to attaining the best possible attitude of the boat's hull, and are widely held to increase the boat's speed as well as improving the ride. They can be manually adjusted or hydraulically from the boat's helm.

Small Boat Electrics

Many small boats are used quite satisfactorily with no electrical power at all aboard, but if you wish to run an echo-sounder, VHF, CB radio, lights, live-bait aerators and so on, then a battery and some means of electrical distribution are desirable.

Batteries for use on small boats can be divided into two basic types. The most common type is the car battery which is used to start engines. The other type is the 'deep cycle' battery used for lighting and today's increasingly complex on-board electronics. These batteries differ in their construction in that a car battery has thinner plates and more of them to deliver the high amps necessary to kick a cold engine over. A 'deep cycle' battery, even though it might be rated at the same amp/hour capacity as a car battery, cannot deliver the same kick, but it will deliver its power for much longer.

What sort of battery you choose depends on your particular requirements. In a small fishing dinghy, even though you may have a manual-start engine, you may well require a battery to run your echo-sounder, radio and so on, and for such light duties the much cheaper car battery will give satisfactory performance provided you keep it well charged. My battery is identical to the one in my car and I swap them over occasionally, as well as charging them off my outboard. It seems to work quite well.

Keep your batteries clean and as dry as possible and make sure all the connections are periodically cleaned and smeared with a coat of grease to keep the corrosive effects of salt water at bay. You can check your battery's state of charge with either a hydrometer or a simple voltmeter. It pays to keep a keen eye on the charge, otherwise you will be disagreeably surprised how quickly the battery will become unserviceable.

Most inboard engines will have a dynamo or alternator to charge the battery as you motor along and many of today's larger outboards have such a generator as standard. They are also available as an accessory to fit many of the smaller outboards and it is worth considering investing in one.

Installing electrics in a small boat is not nearly as difficult as it might seem. First decide where you are going to situate the battery, and then plan the cable route to the battery from the engine's charging unit, so that as you motor along you are charging the battery. If you are using a car battery in a small boat the type that is sealed for life and requires no maintenance is best. It is unlikely that you will overcharge this type of battery from an outboard charging unit, and you certainly will not suffer from any splashes of acid in rough weather. Heavy-duty plastic battery boxes are available from chandlers in which batteries can be kept, and some of these boxes have small sockets built in so that your VHF, echo-sounder, CB radio, etc., can be plugged in directly with the minimum of additional wiring.

What many people do is to run another cable from the battery to a sheltered convenient spot – for example, in a cuddy or on a steering console – and then install a block of small two-pin plugs. My small block has provision for four plugs to take radio, echo-sounder, live-bait aerator pump and lights. Although the block and plugs are not really intended for marine use, spraying them regularly with WD40 has made them last very well.

My electrical set-up may not suit the purist, but it is simple, it works and it is easily renewable should it deteriorate.

Lighting

In British waters boats of under 23 ft (7 m) are only required to show an all-round white light at night, but it is recommended whenever possible that they also show port and starboard sidelights – green to starboard (right), red to port (left). It has become standard practice among anglers, if the boat has a cabin or dodger, to show sidelights as well as an all-round white light. If the boat is an open or trailered boat with just a rudimentary dodger, then just the all-round white light is more usual. In practice the small inshore angling dinghy or superdinghy of under 20 ft (6 m) will probably just show an all-round white light which is likely to be bright enough to provide working light, as well as fulfilling its legal requirement.

If night fishing is done only very occasionally then installing lights as a permanent fixture is an expense best avoided. With a simple electrical distribution system as described above installed, then the use of a simple plug-in light such as a car reversing lamp mounted on a removable mast is standard practice. If no such power is available, a variety of battery-operated lamps can be used for this purpose. These are more than adequate, a set of batteries lasting many hours.

Gas lamps and pressurized paraffin lamps provide a tremendous spread of light and I have on occasion used them in my own boat, because there is little doubt that this spread of light attracts the fish to the surface. However, it must be stressed that they are not the safest of lights to use in a small boat, and it has to be a calm, still night before I will take my Tilly lamp afloat.

TRAILERS

Trailing a fishing dinghy is becoming increasingly popular among the ever-growing number of small boat anglers, and is indeed part of the attraction of owning a small boat. The road-towed dinghy gives you a real sense of freedom, allowing you to move from one venue to another, often many miles apart, perhaps following a species on its migratory route, or enabling you to fish for species which are not so prolific on your regular patch.

A trailer also allows you to take the boat home. Apart from being especially attractive to anglers who do not live beside the sea, this also allows essential maintenance or modifications to be carried out more conveniently at home. Also, the boat can be loaded up ready to go at a few minutes' notice, with the engine, radio, echo-sounder, and so on all connected, tested and working before the boat gets anywhere near the water.

Unfortunately, most of us do not have this sort of room available and have to keep the boat and trailer in a boat park, usually adjacent to a marina launching slip. This has its advantages as well as its disadvantages, the main drawback being that everything that can be removed should be removed and taken home, otherwise someone else will remove it when you are not about. It is an unfortunate fact of life that where you find boats you will find thievery – a sad reflection on the times in which we live. Everything you can do to foil the thief is effort well spent, for having your belongings insured is

My own boat, an Orkney Fastliner 19, being launched from the slip at Queen Anne's Battery, Plymouth. My friend Trevor Roberts removes the webbing straps securing her to the trailer. VHF Bluefin, *give me a call on Channel 10 if you are in the Plymouth area.*

little consolation for the heartache and inconvenience caused by theft.

For use when your engine is left on the trailer, particularly while in transit, there is a highly effective locking device which immobilizes the clamp screw levers with a heavy metal tube and padlock. The trailer itself should also be immobilized, and there are various devices available for this – for example, a long-shanked brass padlock which passes through the towing ball coupling or a removable metal ball which locks with a key into the towing hitch. My own solution is somewhat more direct: a length of chain and a padlock are probably as effective as some of these ingenious and expensive anti-theft gadgets, the chain being simply wrapped around and through the towing hitch handle as well as around any other fixed object which presents itself.

In Britain we are fortunate to have several

Strip out and clean the wheel bearings on your trailer periodically, especially if they have been immersed in salt water. Reassemble and repack with the grease recommended by the manufacturer.

excellent manufacturers making trailers in an enormous variety of configurations to suit just about any small boat ever made. If your boat is a well-known make, often the boat-builder or dealer will recommend a trailer which seems to have been custom-built for your hull shape, and this will make launching and recovery of your boat easy in most conditions. Otherwise a walk around the boat-park will soon show you which make and size of trailer will best suit your boat. A few words with other owners will give you an insight into which makes will rot after immersion in salt water and which will last. Remember that the cheapest if not always so in the long run!

Before you choose a trailer it is worth buying the 'INDISPENSION' catalogue which, as well as containing thousands of parts for build-it-yourself trailers, also has sections dealing with trailer design and maintenance, the latest information concerning 'on the road' lighting, and so on.

If your trailer is used regularly as opposed to, say, an annual launch and end-of-season recovery, then a ratchet winch to haul your boat up onto the trailer is a worthwhile investment. Not only does a winch make single-handed launch and recovery feasible, but even with two of you the winch saves a lot of effort.

When your boat is on the trailer make sure the keel sits firmly on the rollers, the hull is well supported by pads or rollers, and that the hull is pulled up tight to the bow support post. A snubbing chain passed through the stem eye, then around the winch to take the strain from the winch rope or cable, is a sensible precaution on long trips. This snubbing chain is a double insurance: first it will save your winch rope from premature failure and secondly your boat will not slide off the trailer at 50 mph if something does break. The hull should also be held down on the trailer with wide nylon webbing straps, so that it cannot bounce about and become damaged while being towed.

Make sure before you move off onto a public road that all car functions are faithfully dupli-cated on your trailer lighting board; also that your outboard propeller is covered by a brightly coloured bag with reflective strip sewn to it. Check that there is sufficient clearance between the road and propeller if you are going to tow with the motor in its down position. It is perhaps best if the engine is positioned in its 'tilt up' attitude with a block of wood wedged and held in position between the swivel and clamp brackets with a bungee cord or a length of nylon rope. The wood will absorb the bumping and banging that the motor is inevitably subjected to while being trailered in position.

Launching and recovering a boat onto a trailer is much more easily accomplished if there are two of you, indeed part of the camaraderie of small boat anglers is forged on the launching slip, where helping others is the rule rather than the exception.

A 25 ft (7·5 m) length of ⅜ in (1 cm) diameter good quality nylon rope is a useful accessory when visiting other launch slips. Often slips are shallow with an angle of incline much more suited to sailing-dinghy launching trolleys than full-sized road trailers. After you have backed the trailer and car down the slip as far as the car can go, often the boat is half in and half out of the water. Tie one end of the rope to the trailer, unhitch the trailer from the car and take a couple of turns of the rope around the car's towing hitch. The trailer can now be gently lowered back until the boat floats free. Fasten the rope and *gently* drive the car up the ramp until the trailer is out of the water, reconnect the trailer to the hitch and drive away to the trailer park.

This procedure is reversed when recovering the boat, but remember when towing it out of the water that this time the strain on the rope will include the weight of the boat, and drive out *gently*. Make sure your knot will hold firm yet is easily untied with wet, cold hands. A couple of wood blocks are useful for chocking the trailer wheels while the rope is undone and the car backed down to the hitch.

As the trailer is continually going in and out of salt water inevitably the painted or galvanized protective finish will take a number of bumps and bashes, so time must be devoted to maintenance. The following maintenance checklist can be easily followed and will keep your trailer in a functional state.

1   Keep an eye on the condition of the winch rope or cable. If you use rope look out for fraying and rust impregnation, both of which can seriously weaken rope. A wire cable should be checked regularly for strands that have become broken and kinked. If you suspect that all is not well never hesitate to replace defective wire or rope. After all, your boat is a far more expensive commodity.

2   When rust occurs, wirebrush it on a dry day, treat with a rust-kill solution such as 'Neutra-Rust' and then paint over with an aluminium or zinc-based paint.

3   Periodically pump grease into the wheel bearings, especially before any long journey. Annually strip wheel bearings and wash out with paraffin. Repack bearings with saltwater-resistant, marine-grade grease. Keep the tow hitch, jockey wheel assembly, etc. oiled and greased as necessary.

4   Periodically check nuts and bolts for tightness. If assembling them from new, use Loctite 'Screwloc', which will help prevent them working loose as well as stopping the ingress of salt water. Make sure that nuts and bolts are either greased or well painted over.

5   Inspect the trailer tyres carefully, since salt water soon perishes the rubber, checking for splits, cracks and the like, which could cause a nasty blowout. Paint the tyres with tyre black, to help keep the sidewalls supple. Pump the tyres up occasionally, especially if the boat is going out on the road after several months at the boat-park.

6   When you wash your boat down with fresh water, hose the trailer as well.

7   Spray trailer board electrical connectors with WD40, and be sure to seal any holes, cable runs and other small gaps with marine mastic compound.

8   Carry spare bulbs for the trailer board. Lightly grease the base of the bulbs with Vaseline before installation to ensure they do not corrode permanently into their sockets.

CHAPTER TWO

SAFETY AT SEA

This chapter is an inventory of essential equipment, much of which is concerned with minimizing the risk of mishaps at sea.

Some of the new generation of super-dinghies have lockable compartments in which items of equipment can be safely stowed, but most small dinghies are devoid of such luxury, and everything of value has to be removed at the end of the day's fishing. A consequence of this is that items like the compass and echo-sounder are installed in such a way as to facilitate easy removal. Many manufacturers are aware of this need and make special 'clip in, unclip out' mounts for this sort of equipment. If you can afford these quick-release mounts they are a worthwhile addition to the ever-essential compass and hi-tech gadgets which we anglers have taken to with such unbridled enthusiasm.

Compass

Anglers in small boats who rarely go out of sight of land have been known to be a bit reluctant to spend money on a compass. But, to be rational about it, there is no excuse at all for putting to sea without a compass. When a bank of fog rolls up on you it can be an uncannily disorientating experience: your senses tell you one direction but the compass points in another, and it is always the compass that is correct. It will get you home if you know how to use it, and trust it.

Navigation-chart and compass work is a skill. We inshore anglers need not delve too deeply into the intricacies of 'blue-water' navigation, but nevertheless a working knowledge of it can confer more benefits than simply being able to find your way home on a foggy day. However, more about that later.

Compasses vary in price from tens to hundreds of pounds, but what is required in an angling dinghy is a small, robust compass that can easily be removed and taken home for safe keeping. Preferably the compass should be of a type that can also be used as a 'hand bearing' compass to take bearings from prominent shore marks, as a method of finding a prime fish-holding reef or sandbank – again and again! This type of compass can often be fitted in a variety of different ways so that the magnetic fields generated by metallic objects such as radios and echo-sounders do not introduce errors into the compass reading. One of my friends lost his boat, and nearly his life as well, simply by putting a small transistor radio too close to his compass. Over a 12-mile (19 km) run he was 1½ miles (2·5 km) away from the landfall which he had made many times before – a salutary lesson to us all.

A good compass is a useful tool as well as a potential lifesaver. You cannot go wrong by doubling the price you first thought of and spending the full amount on a really good compass. An item such as this cannot be too good if your life depends on it.

Warning Signals

Foghorn

The ideal foghorn for the small angling boat is the compressed-gas cylinder with a screw-on plastic horn. The can is about the size of a shaving cream or furniture polish canister. With the plastic cone in place it is a useful one-handed horn, which should be sounded once every two minutes if you are under way and twice every two minutes if stationary in fog.

Small foghorns of this type are not expensive and, provided you keep the canister clean, dry and free from rust, will last several years if not used. If you have had to use the horn make sure you obtain a spare canister, so that you do not run out of gas just as you see a large shape materializing out of the mist. Give the canister a good shake before using or testing it. Always test it out of doors, unless you want every other inhabitant of your house to levitate with fright.

Flares

Flares come in two basic colours, red and white. If you fire a red flare its meaning is very clear: 'My life is in danger, please come and help me!' It is as simple as that, and so firing a red flare is not to be undertaken lightly, because all who can will come to your assistance.

By putting up a white flare you indicate to another vessel that it is on a collision course with your boat, perhaps because your engine has conked out. At the same time sound your foghorn so that you issue a warning to both eyes and ears. According to the *Seaway Code* published by HM Coastguard small craft within 3 miles (5 km) of the shore should carry two red flares and two orange position-indicating

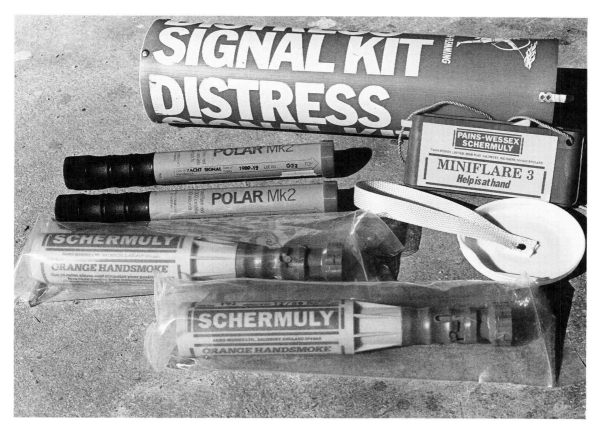

Safety at Sea does not come cheap! The minimum flare requirement for an inshore angling boat should be two red flares and two orange handheld smoke flares.

smoke flares, as well as white flares. This should be taken as the minimum requirement, and aboard a small dinghy which frequently goes outside the sheltered waters of the harbour, it would be a good idea to include one or two of the more powerful two-star red signal flares or even one or two parachute flares.

If in trouble, fire these powerful flares first to draw attention to yourself. If the Coastguard has spotted you he will reply by firing off a white four-star rocket at night or an orange smoke signal during daylight. Your orange smoke signals are a position-indicating distress signal, particularly useful for alerting Search and Rescue (SAR) helicopters.

Another wise investment is a personal pack of mini-flares. These are small red flares fired into the air by means of a plastic launcher which comes with the mini-flares. The intention of these small flares is to provide a personal distress signal – for example, if you fell overboard in a rough sea or you were a diver who came up some distance away from his base vessel. Mini-flares are not intended to replace the larger and more powerful range of full-sized flares, which can be seen over a much greater range.

Hints on using flares

1   Keep all flares in a waterproof container strong enough to withstand moderate abuse. Inspect flares at regular intervals for any sign of deterioration.

2   Replace flares after the expiry date stamped on each flare or sooner if they show signs of deterioration.

3   Contact the Coastguard for disposal of time-expired flares. Alternatively, dispose of them in a well-weighted packet when on a deep-water charter trip.

4   Use an orange smoke flare in good conditions and visibility.

5   Use red handflares in darkness, poor visibility or deteriorating conditions.

6   Do not fire flares into the wind. Smokes and flares should always be fired off downwind. Fire rockets at a 45-degree angle downwind in conditions of low cloud.

7   Take time to read and understand all instructions printed on your various pyrotechnic signals. A crisis is the wrong time to start reading instructions.

8   If you are in real trouble in fog, and you can hear the helicopter or other vessel, fire a flare. Their radar will 'see' the magnesium contained in the flare.

Oars and rowlocks

On a small boat, oars are an important secondary means of propulsion. Not only do they perform this essential safety function, they can also be an effective means of creeping the boat quietly down on a shoal of bass or mullet, or gently trolling a lure or two across a reef.

Make sure when you are sitting centrally on the middle thwart that the rowlocks are positioned to give you a comfortable rowing position, and that the oars are long enough so that the blades are covered without your having to reach into an unnatural posture to make any headway. In an average size dinghy with a 6-ft (2 m) beam, oars of 8½–9 ft (2·5–2·75 m) are about right. Oars of this length can be a nuisance, seemingly taking up a disproportionate amount of room. Nevertheless, this inconvenience is well worth suffering should your engine fail.

Metal rowlocks are stronger than the plastic versions and are to be preferred, especially if two of you are rowing side by side.

ANCHORS

For the average pleasure-boater or yachtsman going to anchor usually simply means dropping the anchor over the side and staying more or less in the area where the anchor finds the sea bed. But for the angler who really wants to catch fish and whose motto might be 'Put the right bait in the right place at the right time', going to anchor is much more of a science; indeed to position the boat precisely may require two anchors.

The angler's choice of anchor is governed by a set of variables not all of which can be found in textbooks and manuals. Appreciation of local conditions and species of fish combine with practical knowhow and imagination to produce some inventive solutions to a given set of circumstances. The purists of the boating world may look askance, but as anglers we applaud such solutions.

Anglers who fish from larger boats of 20 ft (6 m) or longer are more likely to use anchors of conventional design, with perhaps a three- or four-pronged 'grape' (grapnel) anchor for rock fishing or 'graping right into' a wreck, should this specialized wreck-fishing technique be called for.

Anchors and anchoring techniques for use with small boats are often unconventional, and

we might conclude that this could be one of the reasons for the disproportionate success enjoyed by many small boat anglers. Let us look first at conventional anchors, and then at a couple which are unconventional in the way they are used and often lost.

The price of conventional anchors bought from a chandler is horrendous – a symptom of a system which charges not according to worth but to what it can get from its yellow-wellied clientele. So do not be afraid to have a go at making your own, experimenting with different shapes and sizes, hiring a welding plant for a day may well save you many pounds for years to come.

The rule of thumb governing the weight of an effective anchor is a pound (0·5 kg) for every foot (30 cm) of boat length.

'Tripping an anchor' means that it is fastened 'fore and aft', with the anchor chain being shackled to the fluke (barb) end of the anchor.

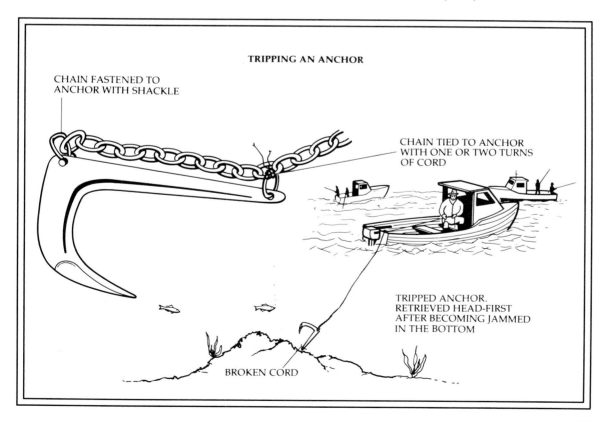

TRIPPING AN ANCHOR

CHAIN FASTENED TO ANCHOR WITH SHACKLE

CHAIN TIED TO ANCHOR WITH ONE OR TWO TURNS OF CORD

TRIPPED ANCHOR. RETRIEVED HEAD-FIRST AFTER BECOMING JAMMED IN THE BOTTOM

BROKEN CORD

The chain is then tied to the shank end with a specific number of turns of weaker twine. Should the anchor become jammed in rock, then by the application of more than normal anchoring strain the anchor will 'trip', breaking the twine and allowing the anchor to be reversed out of whatever is jamming it in. At least that is the theory, and most times this method works well enough. Occasionally, however, no matter what you do your anchor will not come out. If you are in shallow water, and it is warm, it is no great problem to go over the side and pull yourself down the rope to free the anchor. Otherwise buoy the rope off and go in search of one of the many divers who haunt the coastline almost as much as we anglers do. Generally they are most obliging and make no great thing of freeing an anchor for you – a beer or two at the end of the day is usually enough thanks.

Anchor chain

In order for an anchor to bite effectively the pull must be as near horizontal as possible. A length of chain is connected to the anchor in order to minimize the lifting effect of the rope, and any pull on the anchor must first lift the length of chain before it can have any effect on the anchor.

The length of chain used depends largely on the size of boat and the sea conditions. My experience with my own small boat suggests that 10–12 ft (3–3·5 m) of ¼ in (5 mm) steel chain (the second measurement refers to the diameter of the metal used to make the chain links) will easily hold a heavy 15-ft (4·5 m) dinghy in most conditions. If this length of chain does not hold your anchor on a rough day, then a heavy weight such as a sash weight, slid down the anchor rope until it is stopped by the chain shackle, will effect an immediate improvement.

The length of the anchor rope is determined by the depth of water which you normally fish and anchor in. A rule of thumb is to allow three times this depth as the anchor rope length.

Lifting the anchor

In inshore waters lifting the anchor is usually just a matter of heave-ho over the bow roller and up comes rope, anchor and chain. On the occasions when the weather-gods smile upon us and we venture out into deeper water, lifting the anchor can become a tedious chore. In the absence of the winch often found on larger boats, a seamanlike method of making light work of this particular chore is known as 'buffing up' the anchor.

What is required is a 1½–2-ft (50–60 cm) diameter plastic buoy, or 'buff' as anglers call them. Shackled through the eye of the buff is a 6-in (15 cm) diameter steel ring. The anchor rope is fed out through this eye when going to anchor. When it is time to retrieve the anchor, the buff is dropped over the side and the anchor rope securely fastened to a substantial cleat. You then motor up and across the tide so that the rope is kept clear of the propeller.

The buff slides down the anchor rope until it is almost vertically above the anchor and as you motor away this tries to force the buff under, when its buoyancy exerts tremendous lifting forces on the anchor until it breaks out or 'trips'. You can tell as soon as the anchor is free because the boat will no longer be trying to describe an arc around the pivot point of the anchor.

Continue motoring for another minute or so then heave to and retrieve the anchor rope across the surface of the water – much easier than hand hauling all that weight upward. This system works well and the only lifting involved is in lifting the buff and anchor inboard – which is normally best done by hand, even if a winch has been used.

The fisherman's anchor

This anchor is traditionally the 'do all' anchor and so it does to an extent, becoming more effective as its weight and size increases. As a small boat anchor, its best performance is over rock or rough ground that provides it with plenty to snag into. Its performance over sand or

Unhooking a fine bass, caught on a Rapala SL–13S, Sliver plug. This bass was caught early morning, working a riptide off a Cornish headland.

A plaice which weighed in at nearly 6 lb, caught over the Skerries Bank near Dartmouth. Bait was a cocktail of peeler crab and squid strip.

Auxiliary Coastguard Stan Vincent caught this fine red gurnard while using a single hook trace and worm bait on the Whiting Grounds off Rame Head.

21-ft Redbay Fastfisher, equipped with two 40-hp Mariner Magnum outboard engines. This type of boat has become very popular and is a state-of-the-art semi-displacement hull.

A Nab 21 Dory, showing how well the design has evolved to provide speed as well as a remarkably stable angling platform while the vessel is on the drift or at anchor.

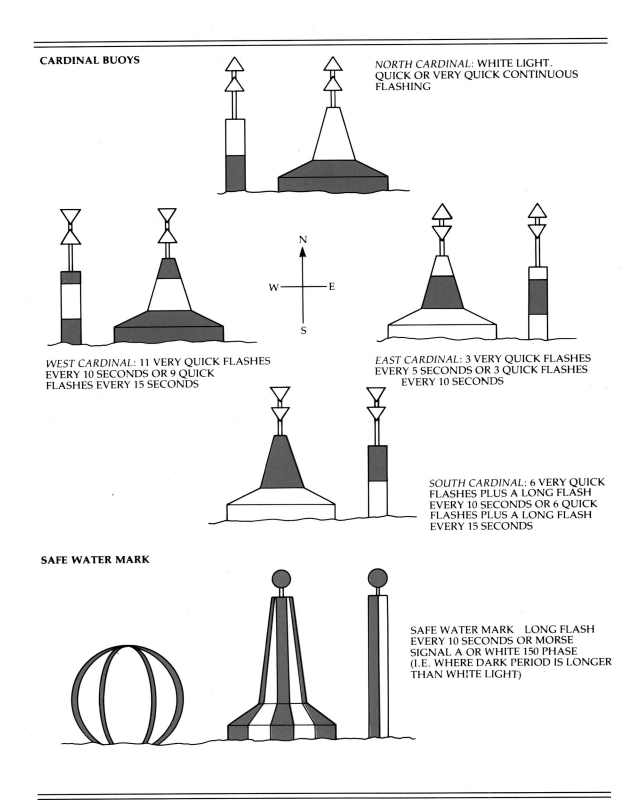

CARDINAL BUOYS

NORTH CARDINAL: WHITE LIGHT. QUICK OR VERY QUICK CONTINUOUS FLASHING

WEST CARDINAL: 11 VERY QUICK FLASHES EVERY 10 SECONDS OR 9 QUICK FLASHES EVERY 15 SECONDS

EAST CARDINAL: 3 VERY QUICK FLASHES EVERY 5 SECONDS OR 3 QUICK FLASHES EVERY 10 SECONDS

SOUTH CARDINAL: 6 VERY QUICK FLASHES PLUS A LONG FLASH EVERY 10 SECONDS OR 6 QUICK FLASHES PLUS A LONG FLASH EVERY 15 SECONDS

SAFE WATER MARK

SAFE WATER MARK   LONG FLASH EVERY 10 SECONDS OR MORSE SIGNAL A OR WHITE 150 PHASE (I.E. WHERE DARK PERIOD IS LONGER THAN WHITE LIGHT)

Rods invariably take a beating and rod rings are the most vulnerable part. Replacement rings are easily re-whipped into place and after the whippings have been coated with polymer varnish, can be indistinguishable from the originals.

A fine wreck-caught ling surfaces after being hauled up from a deep-water wreck not too far from the Eddystone Reef.

My great friend Allan Paddon shows how Greater Launce sandeels can be caught on feathers.

Nigel Miles single-handedly fought and gaffed this fine blue shark not many miles from the Devon coast.

Vic Mozolics and John Loftus proudly show the results of an excellent day's fishing over the Eddystone Reef. Light tackle and Sandeel baits gave a great day's sport.

A superb cod caught from an inshore wreck, proving once more the unerring accuracy of the Decca Navigator in pinpointing these prolific fish holding marks.

A small Orkney Longliner trolls for bass in Whitesands Bay. The birds working over the shoal of sandeels as they are raided by the marauding bass give the location of the fish.

Allan Paddon shows a fine 19-lb coalfish, caught from an inshore wreck using an Eddystone Eel worked on a long flowing trace.

Vic Mozolics fishes from his own boat, the Lancer. *This is a Glass fibre Tamar 2000 displacement-hulled vessel, ideally suited with its diesel engine, for slow speed trolling: which is what Vic is doing here.*

Not all of the joys of boat angling concern catching fish; some of the sights make a day out worthwhile, even if the fish are sometimes hard to catch. The sailing ship Lord Nelson *passes outside the Eddystone Lighthouse.*

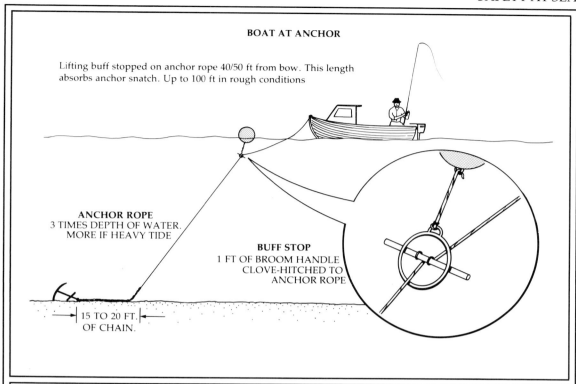

BOAT AT ANCHOR

Lifting buff stopped on anchor rope 40/50 ft from bow. This length absorbs anchor snatch. Up to 100 ft in rough conditions

ANCHOR ROPE
3 TIMES DEPTH OF WATER.
MORE IF HEAVY TIDE

BUFF STOP
1 FT OF BROOM HANDLE
CLOVE-HITCHED TO
ANCHOR ROPE

15 TO 20 FT.
OF CHAIN.

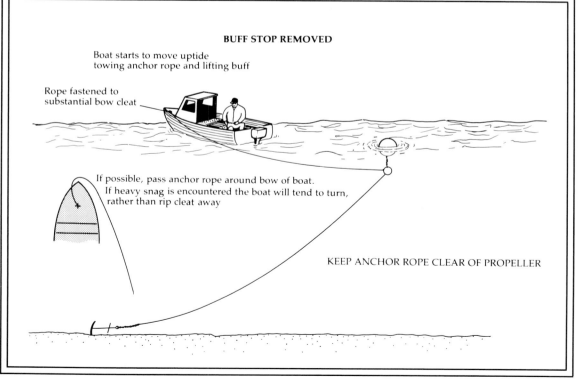

BUFF STOP REMOVED

Boat starts to move uptide
towing anchor rope and lifting buff

Rope fastened to
substantial bow cleat

If possible, pass anchor rope around bow of boat.
If heavy snag is encountered the boat will tend to turn,
rather than rip cleat away

KEEP ANCHOR ROPE CLEAR OF PROPELLER

BOAT TOWING BUFF

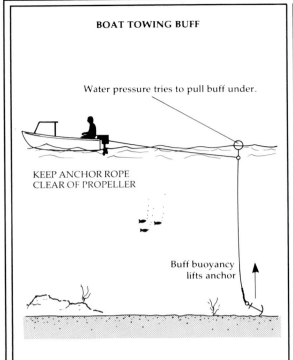

Water pressure tries to pull buff under.

KEEP ANCHOR ROPE
CLEAR OF PROPELLER

Buff buoyancy
lifts anchor

TOWING ANCHOR ROPE UPTIDE.

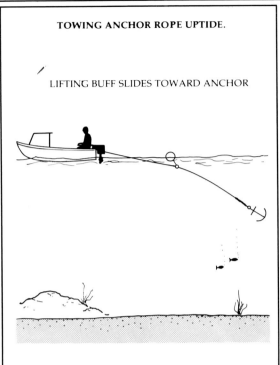

LIFTING BUFF SLIDES TOWARD ANCHOR

FLOATING ANCHOR ROPE RETRIEVED
ACROSS SURFACE OF WATER
No heaving and pulling!

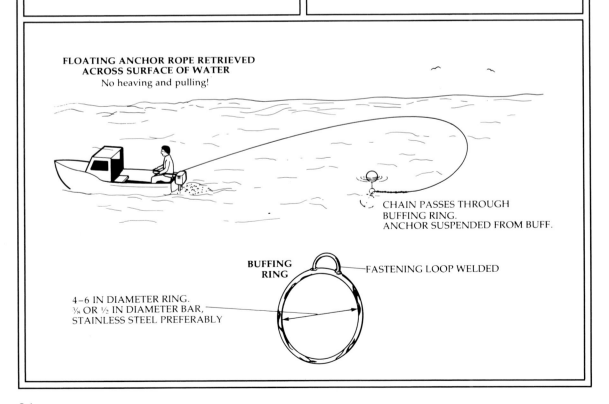

CHAIN PASSES THROUGH
BUFFING RING.
ANCHOR SUSPENDED FROM BUFF.

BUFFING
RING

FASTENING LOOP WELDED

4–6 IN DIAMETER RING.
⅜ OR ½ IN DIAMETER BAR,
STAINLESS STEEL PREFERABLY

mud is barely adequate, and there are better anchors for this type of bottom.

If you decide that you must have one of these anchors, ensure that the flukes, or barbs, have been forged nice and wide so that it 'spades' its way into a soft bottom.

CQR anchor
An anchor that is good in sand, mud and shingle. The pivoted shank helps the forged fluke to stay buried, even if the angle of pull varies. It is reasonably effective over reef or broken ground, but you need to be a rich man to risk one of these anchors over a tangled seabed.

Danforth anchor
This is a very effective anchor in soft ground: the dual spades really work their way in and hold fast. Sometimes even after this type of anchor has tripped, it can still remain buried and can prove very difficult to move. Buffing out this style of anchor is the best method: the action of the buff seems to loosen the sand holding the anchor in. This anchor is expensive to buy but reasonably easy to make for anyone with even elementary metalworking skills.

Bruce anchor
The Bruce anchor is a modern design, originated for the anchoring of oil rigs against the sometimes violent weather they have to withstand. The design is such that when used with a generous length of chain the forged fluke will pull itself in so much that it is said the Bruce anchor has the holding capability of anchors twice its size.

This is a really good anchor but expensive. I have fabricated and welded anchors of this sort of shape, and they have worked well, holding my small boat against some fast-flowing tides. It is best buffed out of the bottom.

Grapnel anchor
The favourite anchor among anglers for reefs and rough ground is the grapnel or 'grape' as it is familiarly known. It can be made at home simply by bundling together three or four rods

of the reinforcing steel used by builders and welding them together. A ring is formed at one end and the legs/flukes bent out from the centre to form an umbrella shape. If a leg is deformed in getting it out of the bottom, it is simply bent back again. If a leg gets broken off, you can weld on a new one.

This type of anchor is good for rough ground, rock and wreck fishing. It will hold firmly yet will easily buff out, especially if the trip goes.

Bar anchor
The bar anchor is nothing more than a length of metal bar with a ring bolt tapped or welded to one end. This type of anchor is used without chain and should be regarded as a 'throwaway' anchor to be used in real snaggy bottoms. If you lose it, it is no great loss, but it is this sort of bottom which often holds good fish.

Over mud this anchor will often hold fast to a surprising degree. Imagine a wellington boot sinking into mud – I think this is what happens to the metal bar. And yet it will easily buff out. Over sand the bar anchor will often roll, giving a stop-start drift which is perfect for flatfish and bass, allowing you to cover ground always with the tide, and always under control.

A favourite anchor of this type was a length of railway line burnt off to the right length with an oxyacetylene torch. A hole was blown in one end with the torch, the rough edges were filed off and a large shackle was passed through the hole. Concrete mixed with scrap iron and allowed to set in a bucket, the loop formed with reinforcing bar like a fishing sinker, provides another cheap but effective anchor.

If you are concerned about an Admiral's inspection, then spend your money on shop-bought anchors and let your boat look pretty. On the other hand if it is fish you are after, do not worry about expensive anchors. Try the scrapyard anchors – they are often just as good.

Drogues or sea anchors
Fishing on the drift is probably the most productive method of catching a variety of fish

from a small boat, particularly when working a live sandeel for bass or spinning over a reef for pollack. Yet such are the vagaries of our weather that on small tides the wind is often stronger than the tide. A direct consequence is that a small boat will be blown along by the wind instead of going in the more predictable direction set by the tide.

The use of a drogue makes it possible to allow the tide to have much more influence over the way your boat drifts. Depending on the size of drogue, it will also have a considerable effect on the speed of the drift. A large drogue under certain conditions will almost stop your boat dead, allowing you to explore the ground around you thoroughly with bait or spinner.

There are various designs of drogue, but the most useful is no more than a square of sailcloth with a brass eyelet in each corner and a hole cut through the centre. The drogue is then rigged parachute fashion with a cord from each of the brass eyelets to a ring a few feet away. From this ring 15 ft (4·5 m) of light nylon rope secures the drogue to where you want it, so that the boat lies at the best position for the sea conditions.

If you get a real 'runner' on, the first thing your crew must do is to haul the drogue aboard, because the fish will try and hide behind it!

The drogue is also an aid to safety in that under emergency conditions deploying a drogue will limit the extent of your drift, increasing the probability that the Search and Rescue agencies will find you within a reasonable radius of where you should have been.

In a buoyancy suit preparing to fire a mini flare; these can easily be carried in the pocket of a buoyancy suit.

Buoyancy Aids and Lifejackets

There is a considerable difference between a buoyancy aid and a proper lifejacket. The latter, conforming to British Standard 3595 (exceeds USCG Type 1 Personal Floatation Device specification), will have a buoyancy of 35 lb (16 kg) and so will be capable of supporting an unconscious person of over 10 stone (64 kg) in the water. It will have its buoyancy distributed in such a way that it is capable of turning an unconscious person face up within five seconds and supporting the head in this position by means of a collar. A proper lifejacket is not cheap but you should consider buying one if you or any of your regular crew cannot swim. Better still, learn to swim!

A buoyancy aid is much less bulky than a full-size lifejacket and as such is much more likely to be worn while actually fishing. However, it does not have the buoyant support offered by a proper lifejacket. The buoyancy aid will probably have a maximum buoyancy of 15 lb (7 kg) or less, and is intended to help an active person help him or herself survive in the water. They are also made in smaller sizes for persons of lesser body weight or children. Make sure when purchasing buoyancy aids that you get the appropriate size for the intended user.

If, like me, you enjoy fishing through the winter, then consideration should be given to a 'thermotic' survival suit, which is essentially a padded overall suit. The padding is buoyancy material so that the suit will keep you afloat, but its advantages do not stop there because it is a well-known fact that as hypothermia sets in, your will to survive decreases. The survival suit keeps your body temperature up, by acting as a wet suit, thereby enhancing your physical and mental capacity to survive. 'Over the side' practical trials have proven the value of this type of survival suit.

Personal Survival

'Luck is good planning waiting for an opportunity.' True enough . . .

To survive alone in the water you must have prepared yourself properly for such an eventuality, otherwise you stand very little chance of getting through the experience. First you should be wearing a buoyancy aid, although even better is a buoyant survival suit (see page 36) containing in its pockets a pack of mini-flares which are fired off in pairs, with at least five minutes between each pair.

If you were able to call on your radio or fire off your proper distress flares before entering the water then someone will be looking for you, the mini flares will guide them to you. A floating strobe flash light tied to your suit and giving off a stroboscopic flash at the rate of 50–70 flashes a minute, is a recognized distress signal and will signal effectively to a searching helicopter or lifeboat.

Probably the ultimate personal survival location device is an EPIRB. (Emergency Position-Indicating Radio Beacon) which is a waterproof, floating automatic radio distress call transmitter. Once you activate such a device, it immediately and automatically begins transmission of a distress signal, which can be located and its position fixed by ships and aircraft with an amazing degree of accuracy. The cheapest EPIRB costs about £90 in the UK and has an active life for about 10 years.

In the meantime you have to survive. If your boat is still afloat, get in or on the boat, so that as much of your body as is possible is out of the water. Avoid wasting energy by attempting impossible tasks, keep calm, do things slowly and deliberately, and keep your head and body covered. Trust the planning you have made against such an eventuality. Before you set out tell someone where you are going and the possible alternative locations. You might also consider the coastguard small boat scheme. Telephone your local Coastguard for details.

First aid kit

Small boats and sharp knives are a lethal combination. A bad cut an hour or even ten minutes from shore can be a difficult thing to deal with, especially if you are single-handed.

A couple of large wound dressings, a roll of 1-in (2·5 cm) adhesive tape, a few plasters and some antiseptic cream or solution should comprise the basic first aid kit. Anti-seasickness tablets, aspirins, sun-screen lotion, a box of matches and a roll of crepe bandage complete my own on-board medical kit. All of this is sealed in a screw-lid plastic container which I always leave aboard my dinghy so that I cannot forget to take it.

Waterproof handlamp

A powerful waterproof torch or handlamp is not only useful for finding your way back to the dock after dark, but it is also a useful safety aid in that it can be used manually to flash an SOS: three short flashes, three long, three short (. . . – – – . . .). Even though the handlamp may be waterproof to the extent that it may float, you should make a regular check on its battery as salt water and any batteries definitely do not go together. Corrosion of springs, switches and bulb housings will soon render even good handlamps inoperable. From new, grease such things as switches and springs with a light coat of petroleum jelly, such as Vaseline. If the lamp is sealed with a neoprene 'O' ring give the ring and its seat a generous coat of Vaseline as well, to help keep the seal from becoming brittle.

Bilge pumps

Some might regard a bilge pump in a small boat as an unnecessary refinement, but I am a little happier to have one aboard. My choice is 1-in (2·5 cm) bore hand pump that can shift several gallons a minute. If you have electricity aboard you might prefer to rig up a submersible pump which will throw the water over the side even more efficiently.

Make sure you have a filter on the end of your pick-up pipe, otherwise you will have things like swivels, beads, and small sinkers gumming up the works of your pump, be it electrical or 'handraulic'!

Radio

VHF

A VHF radio should not be regarded as a luxury on a small boat, and indeed on some parts of Britain's coasts it should be regarded rather as a necessity. With a VHF set aboard you can talk to other boats, to the coastguard – to log out and in and to get updated weather forecasts – listen in on other boats and find out where the fish are and so on. There is also the important advantage of being able to call for help for yourself or someone else. When you call for help on Channel 16, which is recognized worldwide as the open or calling channel, then the whole spectrum of official and unofficial rescuers will come to your aid. It is therefore not a procedure to be undertaken lightly, but in time of need it is good to know it is there.

Two types of VHF set are available to the small boat angler. The low-powered but convenient handheld VHF set comes with just a few channels and just one or two watts of power while more sophisticated handheld sets offer 50-plus channels and maybe six watts of power, depending on how much you are prepared to pay. Providing you are prepared to use these handheld sets with the stubby 'Rubber Duck' type aerial, then they can be enclosed in a totally waterproof, heavy-duty plastic bag, sealed by two plastic strips screwed together with a pair of thumbscrews. The controls can be worked by gripping them, or tapping a touch-sensitive keyboard, through the plastic.

My own experience with handheld VHF sets has been good, and under normal circumstances I can hold a clear conversation from inside Plymouth Breakwater with boats fishing on the Eddystone, a distance of some ten nautical miles (18·5 km). In rainy or misty conditions the range is often just five or six nautical miles (9–11 km) but in such weather it is unlikely that the prudent small boat angler will venture far off anyway, so the handheld has proven itself, at least to me, to be adequate.

However, most small boat anglers eventually

aspire to a full-blown 25-watt multi-channel set with an aerial mounted on the cuddy roof. Under normal conditions, a range of 20 nautical miles (36 km) or more can be achieved. The superior reception and a considerably enhanced audio performance compared with the handheld set is a real advantage, especially with a noisy outboard throbbing away.

Assuming that you have bought a good set and have a good power supply, the next and probably the most important consideration is the aerial. Selection and siting of the aerial is the key to getting the best performance from your VHF. All aerials have a degree of 'gain', which has the effect of multiplying the emitted wattage of your set. Each 3-decibel gain by the aerial effectively doubles the wattage. For example, an aerial with 3dB gain increases the performance of a 25-watt set to an apparent 50 watts. This would seem at first sight to be a great way of making sure that your transmission will blast its way across the airwaves. Unfortunately, it is not as simple, for what happens with high-dB aerials is that the signal is compressed into a long, narrow envelope of emission so that with the boat rolling in the sea the signal could be beamed into the sea or out into space.

The best compromise between performance and practical application is an aerial of about 6dB gain and this should be mounted as high as possible on your boat in order to increase your set's VHF horizon.

Using a VHF set is easy and is something that you should never be frightened to do in an emergency. If you plan to use a VHF set on your boat, you should obtain a Restricted Certificate of Competence. This entails a fairly straightforward examination to show that you understand how to use the set and the proper 'on air' procedures. There are a variety of ways in which this certificate can be obtained, such as courses run by a nautical training establishment or a commercial outfit such as the Radio School, which offers a one-day course followed by an on-the-spot examination. Application forms for this

examination can be obtained from the Royal Yachting Association, RYA House, Romsey Road, Eastleigh, Hants SO5 4YA.

Do not forget that your radio set itself also has to be licensed, although the annual cost is just a few pounds. A Post Office official might also check the installation of the equipment and the set itself to confirm that the licensing conditions have been complied with.

Anglers afloat are inveterate chatterboxes and it is often easy to pick out the operators who are qualified and therefore legal, from those who are not. 'Over and out' is one of the most common giveaways, because at the end of a transmission the proper form is 'Over' when you expect a reply or response. 'Out', said at the end of the final transmission, indicates that the conversation is ended and a reply is not expected. Post Office investigators are known to listen in and a small mistake such as this sometimes leads to an official visit.

What the inexperienced often forget during a transmission is that you have a much wider audience than just the person to whom you are talking, so what you say will be heard by all who are listening on that frequency. A good operator will have worked out exactly what needs to be said before even picking up the handset, then make the transmission following the procedures taught in the course leading to the Restricted Certificate of Competence. The transmission will be kept brief, almost curt, and this is how it should be. Most anglers enjoy a chat over the airwaves, and this is not illegal, but take care not to hog the channel, giving others a turn or the ensuing conversation might well become less amicable.

Pro-words

If you listen to expert operators such as the Coastguards, you will soon become aware that they use certain professional phrases and procedures which make their transmissions succinct and unambiguous. These phrases and procedures are known as 'pro-words'.

PRO-WORDS

Pro-word	Meaning	Pro-word	Meaning
OUT	My transmission is ended; no reply is expected. Only one station need say 'Out', but it is also correct for both stations to say it, so that both acknowledge the end of the transmission. For example, 'Kingfisher Out' is acknowledged by 'Bluefish Out'.	NEGATIVE	No, or that is not correct. Permission is not granted.
		SEELONCE	All stations keep quiet and listen; await instructions.
		SECURITE	(Pronounced 'SEC-CURE-A-TAY'.) Indicates that a safety pronouncement of a navigational nature is about to be broadcast.
OVER	This transmission is ended; I expect a reply or acknowledgement.	RADIO CHECK	Tell me about the strength and audio quality of my signal.
SAY AGAIN	Please repeat what you have just said.	CALL SIGN	A vessel's identification as allocated by licence. Always transmitted using phonetic alphabet and numerals – for example, MABC 9 (pronounced 'MIKE ALPHA BRAVO CHARLIE NINER').
I SAY AGAIN	A response to 'Say again' or can be used to emphasize a statement during a transmission.		
READ BACK	Please repeat the whole of your message.		
I READ BACK	In response to the instruction to 'Read back'.	FIGURES	If data such as Decca numbers are to be transmitted, composed of alphanumeric characters, they are always preceded by the pro-word 'FIGURES'. For example, Red 3.65 / Green 43.38: 'FIGURES, ROE-ME-OH, THU-REE DECIMAL SIXX FI-FE.' 'GOLF, FOW-ER THU-REE DECIMAL THU-REE AITT.'
ALL AFTER/ ALL BEFORE	Identifies a part of a message to be repeated.		
CORRECTION	The last statement or word was incorrect; this transmission gives the correction.		
ROGER	Message understood.		
WAIT ONE	Wait one minute, or period of time in minutes. 'Wait five' means wait five minutes.		
AFFIRMATIVE	Yes, sometimes used in place of 'Correct'. Permission granted.		

THE PHONETIC ALPHABET

The phonetic pronunciation of the alphabet and numerals is an essential part of the skills of a competent VHF operator and will be learnt as part of your certificate course. A recommended book for detailed study of this subject is *Marine VHF Operation* by Michael Gale.

PHONETIC ALPHABET

A	ALPHA	P	PAPA
B	BRAVO	Q	QUEBEC
C	CHARLIE		pronounced
D	DELTA		KEH-BEK
E	ECHO	R	ROMEO
F	FOXTROT	S	SIERRA
G	GOLF		pronounced
H	HOTEL		SEE-AIR-RAH
I	INDIA	T	TANGO
J	JULIET	U	UNIFORM
K	KILO	V	VICTOR
L	LIMA	W	WHISKY
M	MIKE	X	X-RAY
N	NOVEMBER	Y	YANKEE
O	OSCAR	Z	ZULU

PHONETIC NUMERALS

1	WUN
2	TOO
3	THU-REE
4	FOW-ER
5	FIFE
6	SIXX
7	SEV-EN
8	AITT
9	NINE-ER
0	ZERO

Multiple numbers are always spelt out using phonetic pronunciation. For example:

14	WUN FOW-ER
98	NINE-ER AITT
362	THU-REE SIXX TOO
549	FI-FE FOW-ER NINE-ER
62·5	SIXX TOO DECIMAL FI-FE

DTI Radiocommunications Division licence application/information pamphlets are available which contain in easy-to-read form most of the information which you will need to license your VHF. These are obtainable from:

Ship Radio Licensing Section
Department of Trade and Industry
Radiocommunications Division
Room 613
Waterloo Bridge House
Waterloo Road
LONDON SE1 8UA

Or telephone 071–215–2316/2047 – they are very helpful.

CB radio

In addition to a VHF set many inshore anglers use an inexpensive CB set in their boat, and if all you want to do is chat across the water to your chums then CB is excellent. Unfortunately, CB gives you no direct contact with official rescue agencies and coastguards; nor will you pick up weather and gale warnings. It is probably best to fit both VHF and CB – many professional charter-boat skippers have.

ECHO-SOUNDERS

The advent of the microchip has revolutionized the way we fish. For example, on the deep-water scene we now have charter boats which might well clock up 200 miles (320 km) on an extended charter, their ultra-precise navigational aids pinpointing the position of half-forgotten wrecks and reefs. But once on position, the echo-sounding system, be it paper graph or a state-of-the-art colour-screen, reveals the position of the fish and, to the experienced eye, sometimes even the species!

These navigational aids are as yet a luxury. Fishing close in, as we do, many inshore boat anglers rely on positioning their boats by the alignment of shore marks (see page 59). This method relies heavily on a good echo-sounder to pinpoint the fish and the mark. There are anglers of some repute who dispute the ability of a sounder to differentiate fish from the undersea rocks and weed, but the latest sounders are remarkably good, as some of the accompanying traces clearly show.

Four basic types of echo-sounder are available to anglers today:

1   The 'flasher' consists of a graduated circular dial behind which is a rotating disc with a tiny neon light attached to its circumference. The disc rotates at a very high speed and the neon lights up each time it passes the point at which the returning echo signals the depth of the sea bed. So fast is the disc's rotation that the neon appears to be continuously lit at that point. A powerful flasher will also reveal the presence of a school of fish, shown as another, weaker signal above the positive bright signal indicating the bottom.

This type of echo-sounder is reasonably useful as a depth indicator to show the position of reefs, sandbanks and other features where fish are likely to be found, but it is not nearly as good as a paper-graph or video-display echo-sounder. A modern version of this type of echo-sounder is a pure depth indicator, just showing the depth of water as a numeral on a liquid crystal display (LCD). However, this latter type of sounder has only limited uses to the angler.

The advantages of the flasher are its relatively low price, almost zero running costs, small size and minimal battery drain.

2   Paper-chart echo-sounders, like video-display sounders (see below) are available in two forms: the first works in a frequency range of 190–200 kHz for operation in depths to 40 fathoms (75 m); the second works in the lower frequency range of 50 kHz, which gives a better picture in deeper water.

The paper chart gives a permanent printed record of the sea bed and fish, and so is a useful source of data for building up a season-by-season picture of a fishing spot's potential. It is also useful to use as a source of reference when comparing the actual contours found with those marked on a chart. Often productive drop-offs, pits, lumps of rock and boulders can be discovered and pencilled in on the chart.

The printed image from a good-quality paper sounder gives the clearest and most detailed picture of what is beneath your keel and is without any doubt the most useful type of echo-sounder for any serious sea angler. But the clarity of the picture and the ability to study the actual soundings and then analyze your success or failure, does not come cheap. The high cost of constantly replenishing sounder paper is one reason why many of today's anglers look more favourably at the video and LCD type of display.

3   Video/cathode ray tube (CRT) – display echo-sounders are made to look rather grand by their manufacturers. What should be remembered is that all sounders work on the same principle of bouncing a sonic signal off the bottom, and the only difference between any of them is in the way that signal is interpreted and displayed.

The video display can be in colour or shades between black and white. While to see a colour image is somewhat captivating, it can only be as detailed as the limits of its display-tube definition permit. For example, on a 6-in (15 cm) CRT device a good display would have a minimum of 256 × 256 pixels or dots, each pixel or dot being the smallest unit of information which can be displayed on that screen. Manufacturers are working hard to increase the pixel or dot density per square inch, because the closer together the pixels are, the sharper and more detailed the on-screen image will be. One day

ECHO SOUNDER TRACE SHOWING FISH SHOALS

FISH INDICATED BY CHARACTERISTIC INVERTED "VEE" SHAPE
CAUSED BY RELATIVE MOVEMENT OF FISH & BOAT

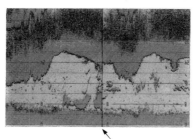

Larger 'blobs' are shoals of
Baitfish – Brit Sandeels etc.

Notice how fish tend to
congregate slightly downtide of
high rock

Use of sounders 'marker' facility

ECHO SOUNDER GRAPH READINGS SHOWING HARD & SOFT BOTTOM TYPES

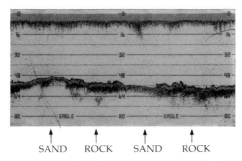

SAND   ROCK   SAND   ROCK

NOTICE HOW RETURNED SIGNAL BECOMES THINNER WHEN THE SIGNAL
IS ABSORBED BY THE SOFTER (SAND) BOTTOM

ECHO SOUNDER TRACE SHOWING WRECK

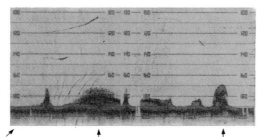

WRECK   WRECK WHEN BOAT IS
DRIFTED OVER

THIS WRECK WAS VERY
SNAGGY FROM SOUNDER
TRACE IT IS LIKELY THAT IT IS
SHROUDED BY A LOST GILL
NET

perhaps this type of TV image might be as good as the paper image. We might even be able to record it onto a video-tape and take it home to show the image on a TV set. There is little doubt that this type of on-board technology is the way ahead, and perhaps the same screen will be able to display navigational co-ordinates, Navtex-type weather reports, the on-board state of play – fuel, fresh water, battery condition, engine temperature, revs and so on.

The one advantage of such a colour display lies in its microprocessor interpretation of the signal. Often the different types of bottom will come up as different colours: mud will be displayed as a different colour from rock, or a fish with a swim bladder will show up as a different colour from a species without a swim bladder. Therefore, although the CRT display is not as detailed as a good paper display, it does show easily assimilated information, which takes much experience to interpret from a paper sounder.

4   Liquid crystal display (LCD) echo-sounders have the most modern type of display. It can be compared to the numbers on a digital watch but on a larger scale. The actual picture relies on the microchip to interpret the signal and instruct the screen what to show. Again the on-screen image is defined in pixels, but the typical LCD screen is cheaper and more compact than a CRT.

The image on the majority of present-day LCD screens is a small 'block by block' display which I for one am not impressed with. However, there are now some which use a very high-density screen which gives a reasonable level of definition, although this type of display is still in its infancy and is without doubt capable of much improvement. The LCD can also benefit from the capabilities of the all-powerful microchip, so it is likely that it will be on a multi-functional LCD screen that we will see navigational and weather data, as well as perhaps a type of digitalized radar. The possibilities are mind-bending!

For those who use an echo-sounder all the time to find those elusive shoals of fish or half-forgotten marks which hold a transient population of fish, the LCD sounder is superb, especially when used in conjunction with a top-class paper recorder. Use the LCD to find the mark, then the paper sounder for a highly detailed and permanent record to sort out the fish from the sea-bed scrimmage. A charter-boat skipper would on paper costs alone probably save the cost of an LCD in a single season.

The LCD sounder is without doubt the way ahead.

Echo-sounder controls

No matter what type of display the sounder has, the basic control functions will be similar. These will be executed through rotary switches or touch-sensitive control panels, depending on the type or make of sounder.

Sensitivity

The sensitivity function can be compared to the volume control on a radio. When you are receiving a weaker station, you have to turn up the volume to hear it. Over a soft, muddy bottom which will absorb the signal, or in deep, water, the sensitivity will have to be increased. In shallow water or over a hard rock bottom, lower settings can be used if all that is required is simple bottom-contour information.

If, on the other hand, you are searching a weedy, scrubby bottom for fish, then a setting between half and three quarters on the sensitivity scale will usually locate them. At this setting a second, weaker bottom echo will be recorded beneath the true bottom recording. This is caused by the echo making a second trip down and up, the signal bouncing off the water's surface.

On top-quality sounders at this setting, fish will record as an 'arched signature' like an inverted vee. This characteristic feature is caused by the relative movement of fish and boat. Inferior sounders will not record this arched signature, and fish, weed and other items often blend into an indiscriminate mass on the screen.

Suppressor control

The suppressor control induces the sounder to increase the pulse length of the signal emitted by the transducer. Most often in a modern sounder this function is controlled by the microprocessor as deeper water is sounded. This control requires some manual input in order to counteract random interference to the signal emission, from, for example, electronic noise from your engine's electrical system, or algae or plankton in the water. Turning up the suppressor control will cause the sounder to ignore these sources of interference without degrading the equipment's sensitivity.

Use the minimum suppressor setting possible, one just sufficient to cut out any unnecessary screen clutter.

Greyline control

This facility underlines the bottom contour with a grey area of varying width depending on the type of sea bed being sounded. A hard, rocky bottom causes the greyline to widen, while a soft, muddy bottom is depicted by a narrow greyline. Weed and such sea bed scrimmage is then shown up for what it is above the greyline.

Avoid turning the greyline control up too far, otherwise no distinct black mark will be displayed: about a quarter of the scale is often enough under average conditions.

Paper speed

This control adjusts the speed of the chart paper or video image across the screen. There are two variables which have to be considered when setting the paper speed: boat speed and the depth of water being sounded.

At slow boat speeds, say 5 knots (9 km/hr) a setting between half and three quarters of maximum will give good arched signatures indicating fish and good bottom detail. In shallow water the paper speed should be about the same, but in deeper water the paper speed can be reduced somewhat. If gaps appear in the recording, slow the paper bit by bit, until a continuous recording is achieved.

These are rough guidelines which should give good results for finding fish. If you are simply looking for, say, a drop-off, then the paper speed can be reduced to give just the bottom contour.

Zero adjust

The zero adjustment is used to adjust the position of the sounder's zero or surface position on the paper or screen. It can also be used to shift the bottom position upward if it is printing too close to the bottom of the screen.

Zoom control

A simple zoom control found on some sounders consists of a switch or push/pull control which enables the sounder to print just the bottom half of the screen contents.

More sophisticated sounders with a computerized keyboard control allow an extremely selective control. By tapping in the top and bottom limits, usually in 10-ft (3 m) increments, any segment of the recording can be enlarged to fill the screen – for example, 90–100 ft (27–30 m) – or to 30–70 ft (9–21 m), allowing a shoal of fish or a wreck to be examined in some detail. Other sounders have a split-screen facility which enables a top-to-bottom picture and a close-up of a segment to be displayed on screen at the same time.

The degree of sophistication that suits your needs is your decision, but consider additional features such as a water-resistant casing, quick-release removal and easy paper loading. Whichever type of sounder you choose, it should be chosen with great care to fit in with your style of fishing, and it should have enough power and facilities to do what you want it to. Remember too that the cheapest equipment is rarely the best buy in the long run.

Transducers

No matter what type of echo-sounder you judge will best suit your purpose, correct installation of the transducer will optimize the sounder's performance. The transducer is both the signal emitter and the receiver, so that whatever form your returned signal is finally converted to, its quality is governed by the transducer's performance.

Installing a transducer

There are three methods of installing a transducer:

1   'Shoot through the hull' is the method most popular among owners of inshore fishing boats. The transducer is glued direct to the hull with epoxy resin, or is fitted inside a plastic tube which is itself glassed or similarly glued into position. The transducer then sits inside the tube, which is topped up with castor, mineral or similar oil.

The transducer is glued direct to the hull or submerged in oil so that the sonic signal emitted by the transducer is not obstructed by any form of air gap, because air will effectively block the emission. This is often seen when going astern: air bubbles generated by the boat's propeller pass the transducer location, blanking out the sounder screen.

2   In the 'through the hull' method a hole is cut through the hull to allow the transducer to protrude into the water. This arrangement is best used on hulls which are exceptionally thick such as heavy-duty wooden or glass-work boats, or if the hull material incorporates unusual elements such as concrete or steel. This is probably the best method, but be sure you have everything figured out before cutting any holes through the hull below the waterline!

3   The last method makes use of a bracket which is clamped to the boat in such a way that a rod with the transducer on its end can be lowered beneath the water's surface to shoot the signal at the bottom. These clamp-on mounts are sometimes called transom mounts, because the clamp is often designed to clamp over the transom cutaway alongside the outboard engine.

This method is usually adopted by anglers who like to travel around and hire a boat for

A basic echo sounder, usually called a 'flasher' because of the quick flashing light which indicates the depth of water. Spotting fish with this type of sounder is often accomplished more by luck than judgement.

their fishing, yet want the benefits of an echo-sounder to help them find the fish.

Mounting a transducer permanently gives the best results and the least problems. The transducer should be fitted in such a place in the hull so that it is looking directly downward. This will probably be close in to the keel where the hull just begins to flare away into its shape. The transducer must also be fitted in such a place on the hull that it has a laminar flow of water past its face, unobstructed by any air bubbles tracking along the hull's bottom.

It is recommended that the transducer be sited in the last third of the boat's length, which is usually the part always in the water. The transducer site can be tried before permanent installation by temporarily sticking a length of plastic pipe to the proposed position with mastic, slipping the transducer inside the tube and topping up the tube with water. Make sure the pipe sits vertically.

If you are not happy with the signal try different sites until you get good readings. In the unlikely event that you cannot obtain a satisfactory reading, get your local marine electronics expert to check for electrical interference which could be causing your problem.

The transducer stuck direct to the hull with epoxy resin gives the most trouble-free results, and requires the least effort. Clean the fibre-glass of grease or paint with coarse glass-paper, make a circular dam of plasticine and fill with epoxy resin, place the transducer in the middle of the dam, pressing it down and twisting, to ensure the face is clear of any bubbles. Rest a heavy weight on top of the transducer to counter any tendency it might have to float in the resin, and leave to set. Make sure you are sticking the transducer to the hull itself and not to any form of foam-filled double bottom. If necessary, cut through the foam to reach the hull skin.

Choosing transducer beam angle

The signal sent down towards the sea bed from the transducer can be likened to the beam from a torch spreading out in the form of a cone. The angle of spread of this cone is referred to as the beam or cone angle. On the low-frequency 50-kHz echo-sounders the beam angle is usually 45–50 degrees, while the more useful high-frequency 190–200 kHz sets usually employ transducers with an angle of between 8 and 25 degrees.

The disadvantage of the wide-angle transducer is that an object on the sea bed – a wreck, for example – can appear to be directly under the boat when in fact, because it is on the periphery of the scanned area, the wreck can be many feet away and your bait is nowhere near the fish – a distinction often not understood by some of the charter-boat skippers who use the low-frequency 50-kHz sounders.

The high-frequency 200-kHz sets are the best all-round choice for the inshore angling boat, and generally come with a 15–20-degree transducer as standard. My own experience with a 20-degree transducer fishing inshore waters to a depth of 100 ft (30 m) suggests that the 20-degree transducer is more than adequate. However, there have been times when I have wished for a narrow-beam transducer so that the sea-bed picture I had on my screen could have been more tightly specific. This facility for using a dual transducer rig is entirely possible with certain makes. All that is required is a 'switch-over' box into which the leads from both the wide- and narrow-beam transducers are plugged, so that by simply throwing a switch on the box, the signal can be switched from the wide-beam to the narrow-beam transducer.

Another advantage of the narrow beam is that the signal is much more concentrated and will consequently penetrate deeper, giving better results in depths which are usually the province of the 50-kHz sets. The difference is rather like that between a tight-beamed searchlight and a photoflood: the searchlight throws its light a lot further than the photoflood because it concentrates the light into a tightly focused beam.

CHAPTER THREE

SEAMANSHIP

We sea anglers are well known for our indifference to the often petty traditions and conventions observed by some of the yachting fraternity. Our boats are generally fitted out to fulfil the function of taking us fishing, rather than being moored at some exclusive marina looking pretty. The angler is more often a practical person who prefers to do his own thing rather than pay someone else to do it for him. So this chapter is devoted to practical rather than theoretical, aspects of the underestimated skill of seamanship.

LEAVING A MOORING
Assuming you have launched your boat from your trailer and your crew then moors the boat alongside the pontoon while you park your car and trailer, by the time you get back, if you have trained your crew properly, the engine should be in the water and ticking over. Probably there will be other boats in front and close behind, so you will need to swing either the bow or stern away from the dock with the minimum of fuss and disturbance to them.

If you want to go out stern first in a small boat, simply let go the stern and tighten up on the bow line so that the natural curve of the bow pulls the stern out, and be sure to use a fender to protect the boat. When the stern is clear, engage reverse gear, tell your crew to loose the bow line and gently motor clear.

Getting away bow first from a restricted mooring can be achieved much more easily if the direction of the tide is towards the bow. Take a line from the stern to a shoreside moor-

ing cleat around and back to your hand so that it can be easily slipped. Let go the head rope and give the bow a gentle shove off: it should swing out into the stream. When you are clear, gun the engine gently to move easily away and get the mooring line inboard as soon as you like.

Avoid making unnecessary disturbance as you motor away from the dock, and stow your mooring lines and fenders ready for your return.

When coming back alongside the dock, get your bow and stern lines ready and place the fenders over the side of the boat. Slow the boat in plenty of time – outboards are not best known for their reversing. Aim to lay your boat alongside the pontoon about a foot or so out, with your outboard in reverse. This is reasonably easily accomplished after a little practice, especially if there is no tide or wind to influence your judgement.

If you have to come alongside the pontoon against a tidal stream, motor in slowly at an oblique angle to it, and when you are a foot or so away your boat should be almost still in the water and your crew ready to catch a mooring cleat. Your boat will now have its bow almost touching the pontoon with the stern angled away a foot or two. Engage reverse gear and swing the engine so that the reverse pull of the propeller will pull your stern alongside: and parallel to the pontoon. Nicely timed, this is a pretty little manoeuvre and can also be used to squeeze your boat into a restricted space.

To moor alongside the pontoon temporarily, use well-secured bow and stern lines. For

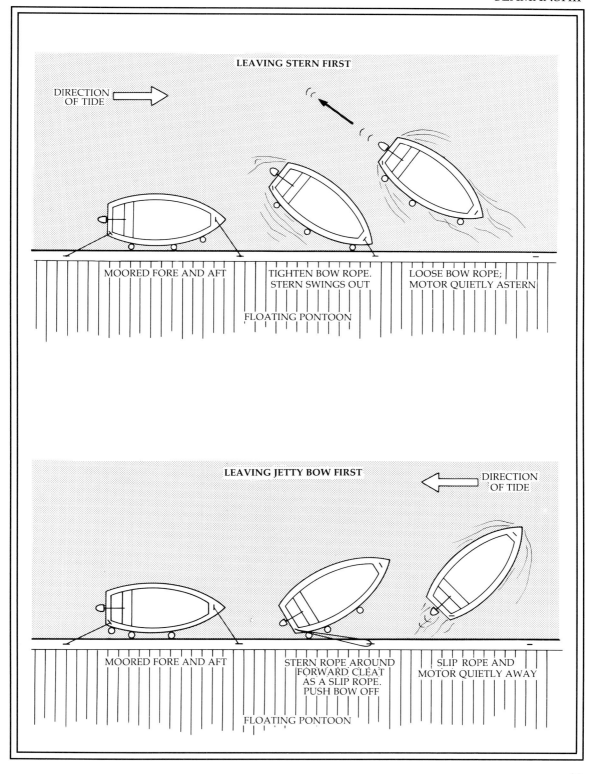

LEAVING STERN FIRST

DIRECTION OF TIDE

MOORED FORE AND AFT

TIGHTEN BOW ROPE. STERN SWINGS OUT

LOOSE BOW ROPE; MOTOR QUIETLY ASTERN

FLOATING PONTOON

LEAVING JETTY BOW FIRST

DIRECTION OF TIDE

MOORED FORE AND AFT

STERN ROPE AROUND FORWARD CLEAT AS A SLIP ROPE. PUSH BOW OFF

SLIP ROPE AND MOTOR QUIETLY AWAY

FLOATING PONTOON

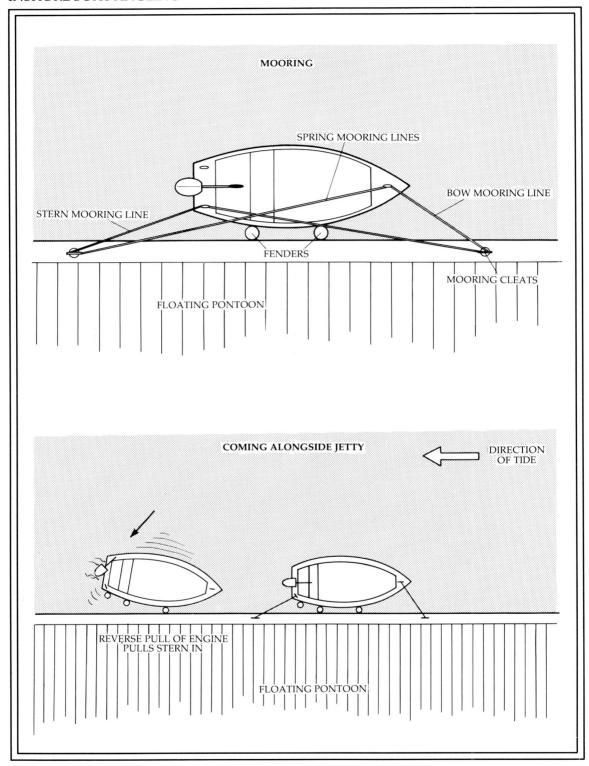

added security on a longer stay, use bow and stern lines and a spring line, to keep your boat exactly in relation to the fenders placed between the hull and pontoon to prevent any damage to your boat.

KNOTS

The ability to quickly and neatly throw a knot into a rope for a specific purpose is a time-honoured maritime skill and I make no apologies for making an effort to perpetuate such traditional skills. The knots, bends and hitches here included are the minimum that the small boat angler should be able to tie. I have not included any splices or fancy work, and if you wish to further your knowledge in this area I can recommend *Knots, Splices and Fancy Work* by Chas. L. Spencer, published by Brown, Son & Ferguson Ltd, Nautical Publisher, 52 Darnley Street, Glasgow, Scotland. This is a moderately priced gem of a book which delves into the age of iron men and wooden ships, and the almost delicate skills and precision then employed in

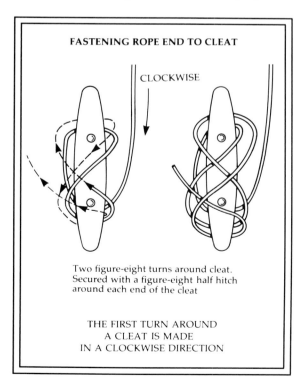

FASTENING ROPE END TO CLEAT

CLOCKWISE

Two figure-eight turns around cleat. Secured with a figure-eight half hitch around each end of the cleat

THE FIRST TURN AROUND
A CLEAT IS MADE
IN A CLOCKWISE DIRECTION

the working of cord and rope. In this high-tech age such low-tech skills as these will one day be classed as an art form. I make no secret of my admiration of these largely redundant but lovely skills.

TIDES

Tides and weather are major influences on the movement and habits of fish, and in turn on the anglers who put to sea in search of sport. Tide tables are available for each area of our coast and a study of these will reveal a two-week cycle of alternating large tides (spring tides) and small tides (neap tides).

Tides are caused by the gravitational pull of the Moon and Sun. One week the gravitational pull is just that of the Sun, so the tide is a neap or small tide. The following week the gravitational pull is that of the Sun plus that of the Moon, so the tide is a spring or large tide. This alternation between spring tides and neap tides and the time of day when high and low tide occurs are vital factors in the daily life of the fish and are of great significance to any angler capable of reading the signs.

It would be quite wrong to assume that the tide simply comes in and goes out, for often, because of local geographical influences, the ebb and flow of the tide will create strong localized currents like a river of movement within the sea. Charts are available that show these localized currents and when used in conjunction with the geographical charts of your area and your own local knowledge, they can provide clues to the location of schools of baitfish and their attendant predators. This research might also reveal the presence of unsuspected sandbanks, holding spots for shoals of mullet and other features. Seeking to confirm your suspicions with your echo-sounder and by actually fishing the spot is one of the greatest joys of angling – especially when your suspicions are proven right.

You will find that on balance most places fish best on the flood tide, the fish following the tide in as it covers rocks, sandbanks and mudflats

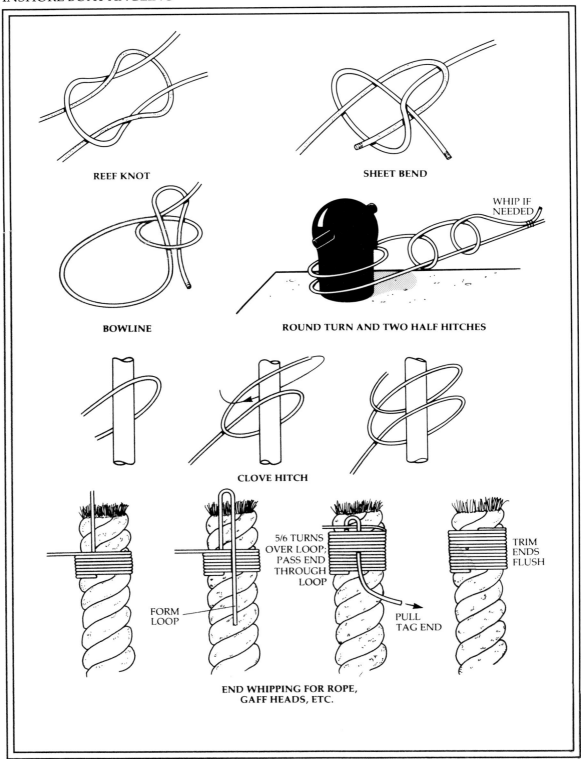

REEF KNOT

SHEET BEND

WHIP IF NEEDED

BOWLINE

ROUND TURN AND TWO HALF HITCHES

CLOVE HITCH

FORM LOOP

5/6 TURNS OVER LOOP; PASS END THROUGH LOOP

PULL TAG END

TRIM ENDS FLUSH

END WHIPPING FOR ROPE, GAFF HEADS, ETC.

and indeed even in deeper water it has been my experience that the flood has produced the better fish.

The ebb tide is not so universally productive, but you will find that there are certain spots and specialized techniques which will catch fish. This is the time to get the binoculars out and carefully study the veteran anglers who have a lifetime's experience to draw upon, because they will catch the occasional good fish when no one else is catching anything.

Very often you will find that certain stages of the tide will evoke a response in certain species of fish. For example, ray and bass in particular seem to feed heavily, and thus are more vulnerable, on what we call the 'young flood' – the first hour or so of the flood tide. Pollack and mackerel seem to be more active from 'half tide up'. No doubt these different feeding patterns among the different species vary from location to location, but they are factual and invite systematic research and study. Indeed a long-term log of tide, time and climatic conditions can often reveal unsuspected patterns of behaviour in the various species.

WEATHER

I feel that the weather plays a much larger part in our efforts to catch fish than most of us would be prepared to admit. Again the long-term log of catches can reveal patterns. From my own rough and ready, often incomplete, and therefore scientifically inconclusive records, it seems to me that the best catches of fish are taken when the barometric pressure is rising or is already high. It could perhaps be said that this is just an excuse for being a 'fair-weather fisherman' – but that rising pressure remains one of my pet superstitions!

'When the wind's in the East, the fish bite least' is another well-known cautionary piece of advice, completely unproven; but several of my commercial fishermen friends are firm believers in the truth of this old saw. Why these things should be is a mystery, and how fish 40 fathoms down know the wind is easterly and that the glass is dropping away is beyond my comprehension. Suffice to know that they do, so that the day can be planned accordingly. And yes, I repeat that I am superstitious – I don't know a true fisherman who is not.

We all have our own little weather forecasting omens, be it a skein of seaweed hanging in the boathouse or the latest in digitalized barometers. What is important is that we can get an accurate forecast from the Met. Office and that we understand precisely what they tell us. The chart below gives the precise meanings of words used in Meteorological Office forecasts.

Visibility
Good – over 5 nautical miles (9 km)
Moderate – 2 to 5 nautical miles (4–9 km)
Poor – 1,100 yards to 2 nautical miles (1–4 km)
Fog – less than 1,100 yards (1 km)

Wind
Imminent – within 6 hours of time of issue
Soon – between 6 to 12 hours of issue
Later – more than 12 hours after issue

Speed and direction of pressure system
Slowly – less than 15 knots (28 km/hr)
Steadily – 15–25 knots (28–46 km/hr)
Rather quickly – 25–35 knots (46–65 km/hr)
Rapidly – 35–45 knots (65–83 km/hr)
Very rapidly – more than 45 knots (83 km/hr)
Backing – change of wind direction, anti-clockwise
Veering – change of wind direction, clockwise

Barometric pressure tendencies
Steady – a change of less than 0.1 mb in last 3 hours
Rising or Falling slowly – a change of 0.1 mb to 1.5 mb in last 3 hours

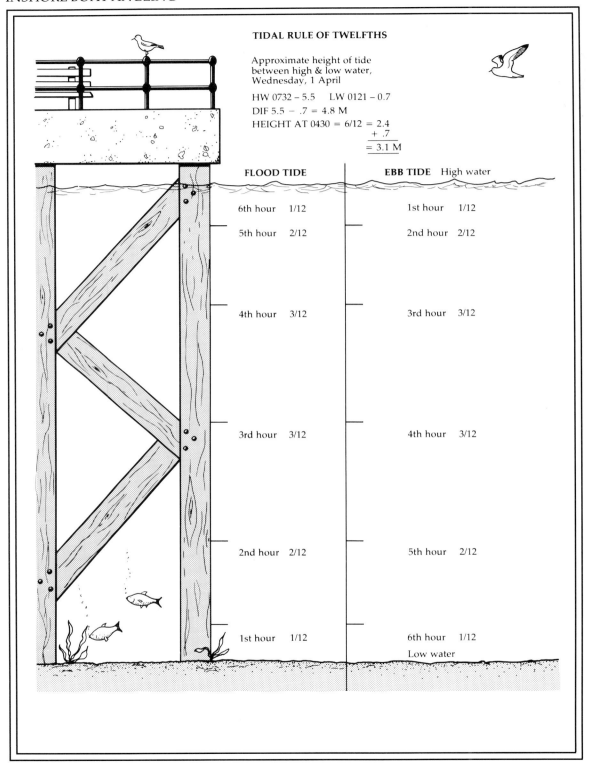

TIDAL RULE OF TWELFTHS

Approximate height of tide between high & low water, Wednesday, 1 April

HW 0732 – 5.5   LW 0121 – 0.7
DIF 5.5 – .7 = 4.8 M
HEIGHT AT 0430 = 6/12 = 2.4
                          + .7
                    = 3.1 M

FLOOD TIDE		**EBB TIDE** High water	
6th hour	1/12	1st hour	1/12
5th hour	2/12	2nd hour	2/12
4th hour	3/12	3rd hour	3/12
3rd hour	3/12	4th hour	3/12
2nd hour	2/12	5th hour	2/12
1st hour	1/12	6th hour	1/12
		Low water	

Rising or Falling – a change of 1.6 mb to 3.5 mb in last 3 hours

Rising or Falling quickly – a change of 3.6 mb to 6 mb in last 3 hours

Rising or Falling very rapidly – a change of more than 6 mb in last 3 hours

Recently the Met. Office introduced its first truly nationwide regionalized weather forecasting network: Weathercall for landlubbers and Marinecall for seagoing types. The Marinecall forecasts are updated twice daily in the winter and three times daily from late spring until late autumn. Giving information valid for a distance of up to 12 miles (19 km) from the coastline, these forecasts use the latest in weather-prediction technology and promise to be of real benefit to the inshore boat angler. To get the forecast you dial the 0898 – 500 sequence of numbers first, followed by a three-digit area code for the location for which you require the forecast. Cards giving further information, plus map of Britain with list of area numbers are available from Weathercall (telephone 071 975 9000).

Weather forecasts on national and local radio can be of exceptional value and a small battery-operated radio costing only a few pounds will serve the purpose and keep you company on long hauls, if you are so inclined. Make a chart showing times of local radio station weather forecasts as well as those broadcast by the BBC. Change the batteries fairly frequently, remembering that dry-cell batteries and salt water are not compatible. An external aerial on the cuddy roof will improve reception, but keep the set well away from your compass unless you want to end up well off your true course.

If you have a VHF radio aboard, coastguard stations now broadcast a weather report on Channel 67 after an announcement on Channel 16, at two-hourly intervals, and will give you the forecast either on VHF or by telephone, on request, so there really is no excuse for going to sea without the benefit of an up-to-date forecast.

Sea angler coast call weather information
Sea Angler magazine, in conjunction with Cablecom Productions, also put out a comprehensive weather forecast via the telephone. This service is specifically for the shore and boat angler, and contains such vital information as wind direction and strength, estimated wind-wave height, swell information, general synopsis as well as specific warnings.

The service is quite comprehensive; the country is divided into 14 coastal areas and all you do is to call the phone number, 0898 600 262. When the number relating to your specific area is read out, you simply say 'Yes', in a loud voice and a voice activated tape will then give you a forecast for that area. The numbers are: 1 Welsh Waters 2 Bristol Channel 3 South Western 4 Central Channel 5 London and East Channel 6 Anglia Waters 7 Humber Waters 8 North Eastern 9 Scottish Eastern 10 Scottish Northern 11 Hebrides Waters 12 Clyde Waters 13 Ulster Waters 14 North Western.

This specific forecast is only available on Friday, Saturday, Sunday and all bank holidays from 0600 hours. On Mondays, a more general forecast is given for the next 48 hours, as well as a long range outlook. There is quite a lot of information given out, and it's worth having a pencil and notepad ready.

Rule of the Road
Small boat anglers are notorious for either totally ignoring the conventions of the boating 'Highway Code' or denying all knowledge of it. My interpretation of these rules is not based on formal tuition but on a practical application of what I have read and observed. Although these rules are formalized in International Regulations, there are times when, for example, just getting out of the way of a bigger vessel is far more sensible than applying all the regulations in the world. But if you have an idea what you should do, the larger vessel, being under professional helmsmanship, will understand and respond properly to your manoeuvre.

BEAUFORT WIND SCALE

Wind force	Wind speed (mph/km/hr)	Wave height	Description	Sea state
0	0	0	Calm	Mirrorlike.
1	1–3/1·5–5	4 in/10 cm	Light Airs	Ripples.
2	4–7/6·5–11	8 in/20 cm	Light Breeze	Small waves.
3	8–11/13–18	20 in/50 cm	Gentle Breeze	Waves, crests not breaking.
4	12–18/19–29	3 ft/0·9 m	Moderate Breeze	Waves, crests begin to break.
5	19–24/31–39	6 ft/1·8 m	Fresh Breeze	Moderate waves. Some white tops. Some spray.
6	25–30/40–48	9 ft/2·7 m	Strong Breeze	Large waves start to form. White tops more extensive. Some spray.
7	31–38/50–61	12 ft/3·7 m	Strong Wind Nr. Gale	Large waves start to lengthen. Foam from wave tops blown downwind. Spray.
8	39–46/63–74	16 ft/4·9 m	Gale	Moderately heavy waves of greater length. Foam blown in downwind streaks.
9	47–54/76–87	21 ft/6·4 m	Strong Gale	Higher waves. Tops begin to topple over. Spray will effect visibility.
10	55–63/89–101	27 ft/8·2 m	Storm	High waves. Heavy tumbling of waves. Heavy spray.
11	64–72/103–116	32 ft/9·8 m	Violent Storm	Very high waves. Extensive foam and spray. Poor visibility.
12	73–81 plus/117–130 plus	38 ft plus/11·6 m plus	Hurricane	Exceptionally poor sea conditions. Extensive foam and spray. Very poor visibility.

I have included the whole of the Beaufort scale although anything worse than a Force 4 wind would rule out dinghy fishing in all but sheltered waters.

Like all good rules the 'rule of the road' is basically common sense, albeit with a nautical flavour. 'Power gives way to sail' – only true if the sail boat is truly sailing. Some sailors with their sails up motor in expecting right of way.

As you proceed keep a sharp look-out, regulate your speed according to such factors as local regulations, visibility, other traffic and weather. Observe other vessels so as to be alert to the slightest risk of collision. Some yachtsmen don't seem to care, so long as their boat is bigger than yours. Be positive in your reaction to a threatened collision, and if need be slow down or stop. If two vessels under power approach head on, each should alter course to starboard (to right) so that they pass port-side to port-side.

When there are two vessels on an intersecting course and there is a risk of collision, the vessel with the other on her starboard side (right side) should be the one to make clear, altering course to starboard to pass astern of the crossing vessel, or simply slowing down until the other vessel is clear. Positive action should be taken early on to make your intentions clear.

In heavy rain, mist or fog with restricted visibility, reduce speed and be ready to take immediate evasive action. Make sure your foghorn works and that you know the right signals:

Powered vessel under way – one prolonged blast every two minutes.

Powered vessel under way but stopped, perhaps listening for your signal – two prolonged blasts every two minutes.

Vessel not under way or restricted in her ability to manoeuvre or fishing or towing – one long and two short blasts every two minutes.

Two vessels approaching one another in such visibility can make their intentions clear by signalling as follows:

One short blast – I am altering course to starboard.

Two short blasts – I am altering course to port.

Three short blasts – I am going astern.

If two vessels are approaching one another, and either doubts that sufficient action is being taken to avoid a collision, at least five rapid short blasts should be sounded.

This is not a comprehensive listing of the signals which can be made with your foghorn, but it is enough to indicate how useful a piece of equipment it is. Don't forget to renew the canister after use and note that a continuous sounding of the horn constitutes a distress signal.

A signal seen more and more frequently is the Flag 'A' International Code which is the internationally recognized signal for a diving boat with divers down. If there is no other way around proceed with great caution in the vicinity of a vessel showing this flag, as divers could be near the surface. Their position is often indicated by a small float or by the boil of air from their scuba sets. The divers are usually friendly and will often stop for a chat if you have the time. Listen well, because they can often be the source of some red-hot information. So look out for the little white flag with a blue swallowtail, painted on a rigid simulation of a flag, and give them a wave to let them know you have seen them.

BUOYAGE

Most inshore angling boats have a shallow enough draught to be able to navigate through what is often only inches of water, in order to get to some spots where fish are relatively undisturbed. Therefore the buoyage of channels, navigational hazards, wrecks and so on is often useful to us for the wrong reasons. But we should nevertheless be aware of what many of these buoys indicate. The buoyage systems around Britain and Europe have in the last decade been updated to the IALA (International Association of Lighthouse Authorities) System A. This system uses five types of buoy, which can be used in any combination:

1   Lateral Marks are used to indicate a safe channel.

Port side (left) marks, to be left on your port side, are can-, pillar- or spar-shaped and coloured red. The topmark (if any) is a red can. The light (if any) is red.

Starboard side (right) marks, to be left on your starboard side, are conical, pillar, or spar-shaped and coloured green. The topmark (if any) is a green cone. The light (if any) is green.

All of these lateral marks indicate the direction of the channel ingoing from a seaward direction, which around the coast of Britain is in a northerly direction up the West coast, easterly up through the English Channel etc. The direction of buoyage is arrowed on the charts and an inset panel such as:

IALA MARITIME BUOYAGE SYSTEM.
REGION A (RED TO PORT).

---

indicates the port's direction of buoyage. It should be remembered that these lateral marks simply mark a safe channel and are no more complicated than that.

2   Cardinal marks are used in conjunction with a compass to show the mariner where to find navigable water or to indicate where danger exists.

A cardinal mark indicates navigable water on the named side of the buoy, so that a South cardinal mark should be passed to the south, and similarly you should keep to the west of a West cardinal mark, and so on.

Cardinal marks or buoys are black and yellow, pillar- or spar-shaped and always carry black, double-cone topmarks, one above the other.

The North cardinal mark has both its cones pointing upwards, is coloured black above yellow, and the white light (if any) flashes quickly or very quickly.

An East cardinal mark has its two cones pointing away from one another, base to base, is coloured black with a single horizontal yellow band. The light (if any) is very quick (three flashes every five seconds) or quick (three flashes every 10 seconds).

A West cardinal mark has its two cones point to point, is coloured yellow with a single black horizontal band. The light (if any) flashes very quickly (nine flashes every 10 seconds or quickly (nine flashes every 15 seconds).

The South cardinal mark has its two cones pointing downward, and is coloured yellow above black. The light (if any) flashes very quickly (six flashes plus a long flash every 10 seconds) or quickly (six flashes plus a long flash every 15 seconds).

3   Safe water marks or buoys are used to indicate that there is safe navigable water all round them, and are often used as mid-channel markers or for landfall marks. They have red and white vertical stripes, are spherical, or pillar- or spar-shaped. The topmark is a red ball. The light (if any) is white and flashes once every 10 seconds.

4   An isolated danger mark/buoy is moored to, or erected on, an isolated danger such as a wreck or rock spike, which has navigable water all around it. It is black with horizontal, broad red bands and is pillar- or spar-shaped. The topmark is two black spheres one above the other. The light (if any) is white with a double flashing rhythm. (For diagrams of some of the marks and buoys, see colour section.)

NAVIGATION FOR THE SEA ANGLER

The sea angler's navigational practice is not that of the oceangoing mariner, but is rather more akin to the pilotage skills of the commercial fisherman. As always with angling, it is the result – and the ease and speed with which that result is achieved – which is important, not the beauty of the method.

It is for this reason that the sea angler has wholeheartedly embraced the modern miracle electronic navigator without any of the reservations voiced by the more conservative among the seagoing fraternity. Indeed, it has reached the stage where some anglers would not know a set of parallel rules if they were to leap off the chart and bite their fingers!

Of course the skilled boat angler has to know the basics: how to read a chart, plot a course, allow for variation and other factors and transfer these readings to his navigator as waypoints, and then how to check by visual observation that he has got it right. I do not intend to turn this book into a treatise on navigation, but a knowledge of this much at least is indispensable for the small boat angler.

First, the method of finding a mark or, more importantly, finding a mark again and again, without the use of electronics or indeed even a chart. This method has served mariners and fishermen well for centuries. It is the time-honoured technique based on the alignment of fixed shore marks. This method is as relevant today as it has ever been, but perhaps what has not been explained except by word of mouth is that there are a few refinements which can increase the consistent accuracy of this age-old skill to such an extent that, if you fish only a handful of marks in good weather, you may well question the value of ever investing money in an electronic navigational system.

The first thing you will need, assuming that you are already familiar with the shore marks, is a good pair of binoculars of, say, 8 × 30 or 7 × 25 power. If you can afford them, the brightly coloured rubber-covered waterproof type are best. Binoculars such as these have the effect of first magnifying the image and foreshortening the perspective, so that when you align your shore marks – say a lighthouse and a tree –then they will appear larger than life and any misalignment is very apparent.

Using binoculars to align two or three such transits (shore marks) over relatively short distances can find a productive mark with consistency. When the shore marks are lined up it is good practice to drop a small buoy to mark the spot irrespective of what shows on your echo-sounder. This buoy or 'dahn' as the fishermen call them, will probably not be exactly on the spot, but once you have used the dahn as a

point of reference in your subsequent search, you will know that it is, say, 25 yards (23 m) uptide of the mark. Then, using the dahn as a marker, you can drift or anchor the mark with some degree of precision.

One of my favourite tricks is to stream the dahn behind my boat as I approach the mark. Then, as I pass over the mark, I deliberately drop the weight a minute or so uptide so that my drift can start from the dahn each time. When you motor back up to the dahn avoid going straight back uptide. Instead, go around so that the noise from your motor does not spook the fish, and be especially careful in shallow water. A good echo-sounder is invaluable, as is a good record of your shore marks. In years to come such a record in the form of a small notebook could be invaluable.

Basic navigational equipment should always be carried, even if you have an electronic navigator aboard. Shown here are the basic essentials: chart, Bretton Plotter, handheld compass, pencil.

Research on a large-scale chart can pay very real dividends. At certain times of the year sand patches can hold transient populations of flounder and plaice as well as early morning and late evening bass. An odd rock can shelter a large pollack or cod, a weeded reef could hold a big old wrasse. There are many such opportunities to be exploited using a modicum of research, a little imagination and some degree of determination.

The chart will also show reefs and maybe wrecks, which are favourite fish-holding marks, often just a few miles from the coast. To find these marks a combination of traditional navigation and lining up shore marks may well work for you in conditions of good visibility, but it is in this sort of situation that the electronic navigator begins to prove its worth.

However, for the moment let us do things the hard way, without the magic box of tricks. There are two good reasons for this: first you may not have an electronic navigator and secondly, even if you do have a navigator it might one day let you down. So the ability to use a chart to plot a course back to harbour is a necessity for your own safety. One of my trawler skipper friends never tires of recounting the story of the 20-ft cruiser which pulled up alongside his vessel some 20 miles (32 km) offshore: the 'danglers', as he calls us, asked which way the land was.

After studying your chart you may well have picked out one or two likely looking peaks of rock or promising sand patches, and the next move is to find them using your echo-sounder and compass. The next part of this chapter will explain in some detail how to arrive at a bearing and a time to steer. Firstly, however, experience has taught me that there is an optimum time of day to try to pinpoint such a mark accurately.

First, choose dead-slack water at the top or bottom of the tide (my own preference is for the latter). Then choose a day when there is very little wind, again my own preference is for about five to six o'clock in the morning, before the wind gets up for the day and when there are few curious eyes about. By choosing these conditions you are far more likely to run a true course and thus find what you are looking for. Whatever happens, drop your dahn at the end of your calculated run and use it as a point of reference to search the area thoroughly with your sounder.

Using a handheld compass

Having taken a bearing using a handheld compass from prominent landmarks, you can, by drawing in those lines on your chart, fix your approximate position in terms of latitude and longitude. If you were a yachtsman making a long passage this is what you would do to establish that your actual position was more or less where you reckoned you should be.

We can also use this procedure to find a mark. We steam off on a main compass heading until a landmark, preferably at nearly a right angle to our course, registers a bearing on our handheld compass, which we had either worked out from our chart or knew to be correct from experience. But do not forget that such a handheld compass bearing would be a *true bearing*, whereas the course we would be steering would be a *compass bearing*. Read the next section, then come back and read this again. By then you should understand the difference between the two.

Chartwork

Inshore boat angling is, by my definition, fishing within sight of land. And yet even fishing five or six miles (8–10 km) offshore with just a light mist coming along and obscuring land from sight, has caused me a few palpitations over the years. So the sea angler should ensure that he knows enough about navigation, and has practised enough, to be able at the very least to find his way home. Besides, the fact that even basic navigational skills will tremendously increase his ability to catch fish is a great incentive to learning those skills.

It would be entirely beyond the scope of this

book to go into the finer points and intricacies of what after all is a professional skill. Instead, let us analyse a typical day out, looking at the practical applications as we progress. If this serves to whet your appetite for more knowledge then there are some excellent books available, such as *Inshore Navigation* by Tom Cunliffe and *Simple Electronic Navigation* by Mik Chinery.

Consider a straight 'in and out' day's fishing: the short passage from the west end of Plymouth Breakwater out to the Eddystone Reef and back.

1   The plotted course from the chart is 204 degrees true and a distance of 10 NM (nautical miles (18·5 km).

2   Variation is 6·0 degrees WEST.

3   Compass Deviation on that heading is 1·5 degrees WEST.

Course to steer is 211 degrees Compass. On a small Angling boat parallel rules are virtually impossible to use, so I use a Bretton Plotter, an inexpensive plastic navigator's aid which is excellent for use in the confined space of an angling boat's cockpit.

Taking the same example:

1   I took a bearing from the west end of the Breakwater to the Eddystone Light. Reading direct from my Bretton Plotter the true course can be seen to be 204 degrees.

2   Referring to the compass rose, you will find prominently displayed a legend such as 'Var'n 6° 35'W 1985 (10'E)'. This tells us that in 1985 the variation was 6° 35'W, and that this figure decreases by 10 minutes annually. So in 1990 the variation will be 6° 35'W minus 50 minutes, which is 5 degrees 45 minutes and to all practical purposes would be regarded as 6 degrees west.

3   Deviation is, simply put, any inaccuracies which will be inherent in your compass, and if you are inclined to go more than say 10 miles (16 km) offshore, then you should have your compass set up by an expert so as to minimize these errors. When he has done his best, he will give you a deviation card for your particular compass. This card contains a list of deviations from the true headings at various points of your compass.

In this example, heading 210 degrees, the compass needs another 1·5 degrees west added to the total to give you a correct heading.

Variation and deviation are added if it is West and subtracted from your calculation if it is East. Just remember the rhyme: Variation West, Compass best, Variation East, Compass least.

In practical terms what we would do is to steer as close to 211 degrees as we could. Coming home we would steer the reciprocal course, which is arrived at by the simple expedient of subtracting 180 degrees from 211, giving 31 degrees. Or as we who make that run on a frequent basis remember it, 'Boiling out . . . Freezing back.' Those of you who are old enough to remember the Fahrenheit temperature scales will instantly recognize the numbers.

While out on the 'Stone, you decide that it is not fishing all that well and you decide to press on to the Hands Deeps, another famous reef-fishing mark, down to the west of the Eddystone. In this case we will not have that superb visual mark of the Eddystone Lighthouse to aim ourselves at. This time we will have to make a timed run on a compass bearing.

The distance from the west end of Plymouth Breakwater to the Eddystone is almost exactly 10 nautical miles and you can check this by using the scale on the side of the Bretton Plotter or by scaling off the distance down the side of the chart using a pair of dividers. Each full division is to all intents and purposes one nautical mile, but remember: only up the sides of the chart, not across the top or bottom. These lines up the side of the chart are the lines of latitude, the lines across the top and bottom are the lines of longitude.

Since distance divided by time equals speed, if the trip from the Breakwater to the Eddystone took exactly one hour your speed would be 10 nautical miles per hour or 10 knots. If it took

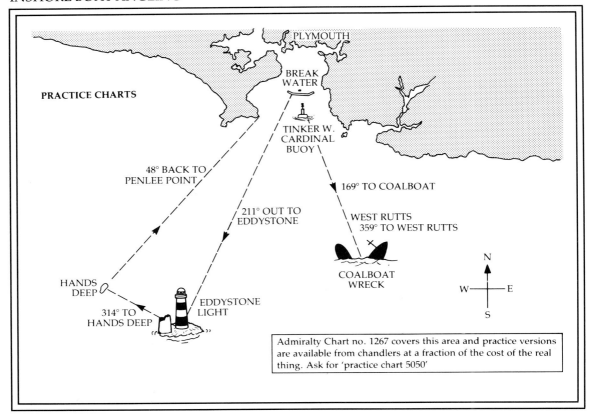

PRACTICE CHARTS

PLYMOUTH

BREAK WATER

TINKER W. CARDINAL BUOY

48° BACK TO PENLEE POINT

211° OUT TO EDDYSTONE

169° TO COALBOAT

WEST RUTTS 359° TO WEST RUTTS

HANDS DEEP

314° TO HANDS DEEP

EDDYSTONE LIGHT

COALBOAT WRECK

N
W — E
S

Admiralty Chart no. 1267 covers this area and practice versions are available from chandlers at a fraction of the cost of the real thing. Ask for 'practice chart 5050'

you one and a half hours your speed would be a fraction over 6·5 knots. But let us keep the faster speed and work out how long it will take us to get to the Hands Deeps. Scaling off the chart, the distance is 3¼ nautical miles. So at 10 knots – 3·25 divided by 10 equals 0·325 of an hour – multiply this by 60 and the time required is 19½ minutes.

Lifting our bearing from the chart gives us 310 degrees true, add to this our 6 degrees variation, maybe take away a degree or two for deviation, depending on our compass, and we have a heading of 314/315 degrees. We now steer on this heading for a little less than twenty minutes and up should come the Hands Deeps on our echo-sounder!

At the end of our day's fishing, we head for home, in this case approaching Plymouth from the direction of the Hands Deeps. Plot landfall to a buoy out clear of the land, or preferably a

cluster of buoys, because then if you miss one you will inevitably encounter one of the others. A heading of 47/48 degrees for just under an hour will bring us back to Penlee Point at the western entrance to Plymouth Sound.

You need not plot these courses and do the calculations each time you put to sea, because it makes sense to keep a record in your notebook of the various trips and fishing marks that you use. Each time you go, little amendments, records of catches at various times of the year and other details will build into an invaluable log of what you have done and where you have been.

Just for a moment, visualize your situation if heavy fog clagged in, your visibility was severely restricted and the weather began to deteriorate. By plotting your courses like this, recording them and practising them on the good days, if and when the situation demands, you will at least have confidence in what you are doing and the direction in which you are heading.

No problems so far, but now we come to the 'by guess and by God' bit: tides and leeway. Let us consider tides first, because these are something with which we are all familiar and there is at least some apparent logic to them. Look at your chart for the small coloured diamonds: these are tidal diamonds, each containing a number. Look for that number in the block of tidal information printed on the chart.

You will see from this information that the tide will set in a particular direction for each part of the tide. You should allow for this tidal push by steering a degree or two against the tidal stream. If the set is right on your bow or stern then it will have little effect except on your speed, and this is fine over the short distances that we anglers cover in our point-to-point navigation. If, however, you decide to take a run across to Guernsey, I suggest you refer to a book on navigation and work out how to make the due allowances. These tidal diamonds have another use for us as anglers: they give us a good indication of the direction we will drift over a mark. More specific information can be found by referring to a tidal atlas contained in such publications as *Reed's Nautical Almanac*.

Leeway is a general term for everything that contrives to prevent us from steering an accurate course. The effect of the wind on the boat or perhaps a tendency of the boat itself to steer off – such things as these you will gradually become aware of and you will consciously, or subconsciously, make due allowance for them.

Traditional navigation is not a mathematically precise art. You do what you can to achieve accuracy, take account of 'what can go wrong, will go wrong', add a pinch of experience and then join the generations of mariners who have all worried about their landfall!

At the risk of repeating myself, I am not attempting to provide definitive information on navigation in this book. If this section makes you seek more information and so become more knowledgeable and expert, then it will have served its purpose.

Decca navigator

The Decca navigational system is an electronic system which interprets radio signals from various beacons around our coast into either Latitude and Longitude or Lines of Position (LOPS or Decca numbers) which in conjunction with a chart will fix your position to a very high degree of accuracy. It is this precision which makes it such a desirable piece of kit for the boat angler because it allows wrecks, reefs and other fishy hot-spots to be relocated time and again.

Until recently these navigational computers were too bulky and heavy to even consider putting into a small boat, but all of that has changed, for the revolutionary silicon chip has reduced the computer in size and power consumption, as well as cutting its price dramatically, to the point where the owner of even the smallest of dinghies with a power supply could have one fitted. It is my belief that with a navigational system like this and a top-flight echosounder small boat anglers in the 1990s are on the threshold of a new era in sea angling. Make room for me near the front!

The electronic navigator

The early Decca sets would have sunk many of the small angling boats that we use today. It is a tribute to human ingenuity that now a more powerful electronic navigator with far more functions is packed into a small plastic box which we can pop into a tackle box and take home with us. It will not be long before we have a multi-purpose gadget which will combine a navigator with an echo-sounder and probably a radar set as well, all sharing a common screen.

So far I have deliberately referred simply to the electronic navigator. This is quite deliberate: at the moment various governments are debating what to do in Europe when the life of the Decca stations ends around 1995. It is likely then that the ground-based navigational system in Europe will be changed to Loran C. This, as far as we end-users of the system are concerned, will just be a different 'box of tricks'. Most of the functions are virtually identical in the Decca and Loran systems and are nothing to be frightened of. You will inevitably make mistakes when you start, but a little practice and study of the manual will soon have you using the new system like an old hand.

Another system in the offing is the American Global Positioning System referred to as GPS. The positional accuracy of this system will be better than that of Decca or Loran and as far as anglers are concerned this is the ultimate navigational aid. So far there has been speculation that the GPS system will be priced out of the reach of ordinary mortals, but there is a strong rumour that one manufacturer is aiming at a price that competes with that of a Decca or Loran set. Good luck to them.

Lowrance Mach 1, paper graph echo sounder. This echo sounder holds a special place of affection among inshore boat anglers the world over. Its competent performance and superb picture quality is the benchmark against which many similar echo sounders are judged.

This is what the electronic navigator will do for us:

1   It will give us a continuous readout in latitude and longitude and Decca, Loran or GPS numbers, of your actual position, to a remarkable degree of accuracy. This means that you can find your way to wrecks and reefs and, what is more important, find your way home again in the dark or fog.

2   If you input the position of these wrecks and reefs, the navigator's microchip will work out the distance to go, the course to steer, how far off course the wind and tide has taken us, what direction and distance we have to move to get back on course, and so on.

3   The navigator's memory will store a hundred or more of these positions, referred to as 'waypoints'. By chaining several of these waypoints together the navigator will remember this combination of waypoints as a 'route'. This is very useful if you are coming home in the dark, because as soon as you arrive at the current waypoint, the navigator will automatically switch over to the next waypoint and show you a course and distance to steer.

Once you are used to the electronic navigator, it is easy to be seduced by its ease of use and accuracy. The traditional navigational skills soon become rusty, and it will pay you occasionally to practise them and use the electronic system to confirm that you can still get it right. But anglers are anglers first and boatmen second; angling boats often carry two or even three navigators, all connected to different power sources and each with its own aerial – just in case!

Fitting an electronic navigator

Before fitting a navigator, sit in your normal steering position and consider the following:

1   The receiver must be easily within reach so that you can reach the key pad to press the keys or turn the knobs.

2   It must be clearly visible so that you do not have to take your eyes away from your forward vision for more than a second or two, especially if your boat is fast. Some navigator displays are of a type which is difficult to read even in weak sunlight, so if yours is of this type, ensure that it is in a permanently shaded position.

3   If your steering position is open to the elements, ensure that the navigator is not in a site where it can be swamped by a wave. Waterproof housings are available for open boats and central consoles.

4   Navigators are a prime target for villains, and whether you are on an isolated mooring or in a marina, an expert thief can remove one in seconds. So either detach the navigator and take it home in your tackle box or lock it away in a built-in strong box.

5   Try to position the navigator away from likely sources of electrical interference such as stereo speakers, ignition components, echosounders etc. Avoid a permanent fixing until you are certain that the navigator is functioning properly.

6   Ensure that your cable runs to the navigator are also kept well clear of the above sources of interference.

7   Try to use a 'clean' power supply, avoid using the same battery which is used to start your engine, otherwise the voltage drop when the engine is started will blank out the navigator and it will take a minute or two to find its position again. I use a separate 12v battery just for my navigator. This is then connected to the motor's charging system for a 'top up' or I take it home and give it a charge using my car battery-charger.

8   Mount the navigator's aerial in such a position that it is clear of any surrounding metalwork, rigging, masts or other obstructions. Try to get at least a 6-ft (2 m) separation from the VHF aerial and if you have a radar set, the navigator's aerial must be above the scanner's beam.

9   Some navigators include a screened cable to the power supply and it is important that this screen is earthed. This presents a problem in a small fibreglass fishing dinghy, but my solution is to take a wire through to the keelband, which, if it is left unpainted, will usually be an adequate earthing point. It is often possible to make a connection to the backside of the winching eye on the bow of the boat. This usually passes through the keelband, through the stem into a backing plate. Simply screw another nut onto the excess thread to trap your earth wire.

10   What is not mentioned in some of the manuals is that your aerial will perform better if it too is earthed direct to the sea. This will give an enhanced performance because of the 'ground plane' effect, whereby the sea acts as a complementary part of the aerial system. If you have a stainless steel 'bridge' over your cabin roof to which your various aerials and navigation lights can be fitted, then a wire from a fixing bolt to your earth point will generally suffice, provided you have metal-to-metal contact between your aerial and the bridge.

If your keelband is ineffective as an earthing point, then you will have to consider fixing a proper ground plate beneath the waterline of your boat. Ground plates are specially made alloy plates which give an enhanced ground plane effect for their comparatively small size, and they are not cheap.

Set-up programming
This is a procedure necessary to tell the navigator the time and day, where it is and what options you want it to run under. For example, you can tell it to give you compass bearings in true or magnetic. Most of today's generation of navigators will work out independently what the variation will be from the initial position which you enter. Some will also accept deviation figures applicable to your main compass, which will be held in the computer's memory and automatically added to or subtracted from the heading which it will show.

The set-up procedure will be detailed in your navigator's instruction manual, but if you have any difficulty never hesitate to ask questions. I have found fellow-anglers, charter-boat skippers, and retailers and manufacturers to be extremely helpful.

Handy hints

Putting a navigator on your boat will not guarantee that you will instantly start catching more fish. But what is certain is that used with intelligence and imagination the navigator's potential to put you in the right spot time and again will tip the odds in your favour. Keeping records is an essential part of the use of a navigator, your 'Decca Book' is used to record your numbers (positions), what fish you caught and when you caught them – invaluable information for the future.

Wreck and reef numbers are kept as secret as is possible by charter skippers, even from one another, and often when you do obtain them they might not be entirely accurate for your navigator and you will have to spend time 'looking' with your echo-sounder until you find the wreck. When you do find it, make sure that you make an accurate record of the numbers and record it as a waypoint. The ability of the electronic navigator to take you back to the same position time and again is its major benefit to boat anglers.

A day out with a Decca set

My electronic navigator is a Navstar 2000, an excellent navigator let down by a display which is almost impossible to read in even weak sunlight, so I stick a plastic or cardboard shade over it with adhesive tape.

On Friday evening I ensure that my Decca battery is topped up and put on charge ready for the morning. Poetic licence allows me to assume that the next morning is a beautiful calm and clear day, and that I can find a parking spot on the quay.

When I press the start-up key on the navigator, it goes through a self-check:

Memory OK

Antenna OK

Receiver OK

Display Bright

50 21·96N

04 08·03W

This last information is the position of my mooring on the Plymouth Sea Angling Centre Marina. Motoring out through the Sound I call up waypoint 05, which is a position 200 yards (180 m) east of the east end of the Breakwater: 50 20·00N, 04 08·00W. Approaching within 200 yards of this position, the waypoint alarm goes off as it should.

Waypoint 06 is a position south by west of the Mewstone, in clear water, well away from the treacherous rocks which surround it. Waypoint 06 is at 50 18·00N/04 08·00W. After a few minutes – its only 2 miles (3 km) from waypoint 5 to number 6 – the alarm tells me that I have reached that position. Next I call up waypoint 20, which is a wreck known locally as the Coalboat, at 50 12·01N and 04 05·12W some 6·25 nautical miles (12 km) on a bearing of 170 degrees, from my chartwork the evening before. The navigator gives me a reading of 169 degrees and 6·3 nautical miles (12 km) so everything appears to be working fine and the boat is motoring along at 14 knots (26 km/hr). Just after I left waypoint 06 I called up the 'time to go' function and it told me that at that speed I had just under half an hour's travelling to do to reach the Coalboat.

Drifting the wreck for pollack with a long trace and light leads is one of my favourite forms of fishing, and using a navigator in conjunction with a good echo-sounder is a superb technique to put your boat over the fish. There is no big secret to it: with your waypoint entered, after your drift the navigator will give you your course and distance back to the wreck, and therefore your direction of drift must be the reciprocal of the course given to you by the navigator. Once you have passed over the wreck on the way up for another drift, carry on the course given for another minute or so. This will give you a chance to get your gear down to the area of the fish before your new drift brings you up on the wreck again.

After a couple of hours and a few small fish, and after a good search of the area to make sure the fish are not holding off the wreck, it is evident that the fish are not in residence today. It is now past midday, so there is not time to go looking for anything special. The West Rutts Reef is not far away and it is probable that the fish are on the Reef somewhere, chasing sand-eel or sprats. The West Rutts is waypoint 19 on my navigator, which gives me a course of 359 degrees and a distance of 1·62 nautical miles (3 km), so off I go. I have been travelling for about three or four minutes when suddenly the Decca screen goes blank. I look shoreward and find that mist is obscuring the comforting sight of the land and all around there is nothing to see

except swirling banks of mist. I have my charts and my Bretton Plotter, dividers and so on with me, so what do I do? The decisions I would have made in this situation are explained on page 125, but first see if you can work out what to do.

Navigating by Decca numbers

The early weighty Decca sets displayed their position by means of three analogue dials: a red dial, a green dial and a purple dial. The readings given by the hands of these dials indicated co-ordinates which, when plotted onto a special Decca chart, would show your position.

Nowadays, for most navigational purposes, the Decca navigator working in latitude and longitude is entirely satisfactory. However, it should be remembered that the set's input signal is still the time-honoured Decca numbers as in those old sets. What actually happens is that the modern set puts the numbers through a

This Emergency Position Indicating Radio Beacon (EPIRB), costs less than £100. It is waterproof, and always ready to start transmitting an emergency signal.

Fixed navigational beacon on the eastern side of Plymouth Sound, marking the deep water channel for large warships making their way up to the naval dockyard.

computerized number cruncher and converts them to latitude and longitude, which is displayed on the screen.

Inevitably, in the conversion to lat and long, the numbers are rounded off to fit the lat/long format, losing some small degree of accuracy. This loss of accuracy is perfectly acceptable for normal navigational purposes, but not if you are trying to find a wreck: the unconverted, raw numbers are the most accurate.

If you have ever tried to find a wreck in the lat/long mode, then you will know how hit-and-miss this can be. Have you ever wondered why so many professional charter boats carry two, sometimes three separate Decca sets? It is likely that one set is permanently set up in the numbers mode and only switched on when close to the mark.

My Navstar 2000 will easily display Decca numbers, if you know how to get them up. The procedure is not difficult. Navigate to the wreck using normal Waypoint/lat long procedures. When near the mark, call up the CHAIN command, switch from AUTO to MANUAL and select the chain pair which is most accurate in your area. It is RED and GREEN on my patch, so I select R – G.

On pressing POS for position, my position is first displayed in lat and long, then in a display containing the RED and GREEN numbers. This page is frozen by pressing ENTER. Your position will then be displayed continuously in the number format, prefixed with the letters R and G to indicate which is which. The Halfway wreck for example, off my home port of Plymouth in the position 50 15·3 N and 4 14·2 W, would be seen as R5·12 and G41·25.

The spatial interpretation of numbers instead of compass headings, lat and long etc., is a skill only improved by practice and experience. Getting a drift spot-on, or putting the anchor in so that the boat hangs just a little uptide of the wreck, are skills of the highest order.

To go home, go back into the AUTO mode and revert to the normal Waypoint/lat/long functions, working the set as you would normally.

This numbers navigation is probably sea angling's best kept secret!

Jayne Hannaford plays a Blue Shark, while husband Grayham is left holding the baby. They were fishing from their own boat Tiberon.

CHAPTER FOUR

TACKLE

Today, fishing tackle is better than ever before. We have rods made from fibreglass reinforced with hi-tech materials such as carbon-fibre and Kevlar, and there are rods which to all intents and purposes are wholly made from carbon-fibre. Most rods are now equipped with light-weight reel fittings and tough durable rings, which, with reasonable care, are virtually indestructible.

The new generation of reels are also made from carbon-fibre and stainless steel, and are equipped with lever-drag clutch systems, which are so smooth and kind to the line that when they are used with consideration and care, line breakages are minimized.

Nylon monofilament technology has advanced to give us line which is smooth, supple, and made to incredibly accurate breaking strains, and with a knot strength of over 90 percent, provided the right knots are used and they are properly tied.

End tackle, such as booms and line sliders, is now made from high-tensile stainless steel or high-precision injection-moulded nylon. New-generation hooks are chemically sharpened to needle-point sharpness and quality control is more rigorous than ever before. It is rare these days to buy a box of hooks and find any with a deformed eye or barbs left off. No doubt fierce competition from Japanese manufacturers has caused European hook makers to set their sights higher.

I do not intend to write extensively on tackle, because it is my belief that method is far more important. But it is essential that as anglers we choose to fish for sport, not to see who can take home the biggest plastic sack full of dead fish. If it is a freezer crammed with fish that you want, then the most successful tackle is a handline!

Rods

Many dedicated inshore boat anglers own a battery of rods and reels specifically tailored to fit the sort of fishing which the season dictates, while others keep it simple with just a couple of outfits – one light and one heavy. For me personally it is not unusual to use a conventional boat rod, an uptide rod and a spinning rod as the day's fishing progresses. Every serious angler eventually arrives at his own preferences where rods are concerned.

Conventional boat rods

Balanced tackle is the phrase used today when describing the relation of a rod's strength and stiffness to line breaking strain and then the matching of this combination to the strength, weight and fighting prowess of the species of fish sought, and the fishing conditions. In recent times this attempt at achieving balance has been advocated and promoted by the International Game Fish Association so that today any reputable boat rod will carry what is known as an IGFA line rating. This indicates the appropriate partnership of rod and line.

In Britain these ratings are still widely referred to in pounds, even though several years ago the whole system was metricated. No doubt we will be into the new century before anglers start to describe line ratings in metric values.

Portable gunnel-mounted rod rests are ideal for static fishing conditions, for ray or plaice for example.

IGFA RATINGS

Old Rating	New Rating	Strength Allowable
2 lb	1 kg	2·2 lb
4 lb	2 kg	4·4 lb
8 lb	4 kg	8·8 lb
16 lb	8 kg	17·6 lb
20 lb	10 kg	22·0 lb
30 lb	15 kg	33·0 lb
50 lb	24 kg	53·0 lb
80 lb	37 kg	81·6 lb
130 lb	60 kg	132·0 lb

This system of ratings may not be of interest to you in determining how you fish, but the ratings do act as a benchmark, indicating the strength of rod you may be required to use, and may help when buying a new rod.

Boat rods have become longer in the past couple of decades and with this increase in length to 7 ft 4 in or 7½ ft (2·2–2·3 m) their action has become more 'tippy' as the tapers have gradually increased with the greater sophistication of the materials and the use of computer-calculated progressive taper action. However, shorter rods using the same sophisticated design and materials have started to gain favour as anglers rediscover the direct power they can apply to bottom-hugging species such as conger and ray.

Uptide rods

This type of rod is used to cast your baits uptide and away from the inevitable boat noise, which without doubt scares the fish, especially in the shallow waters in which this technique originated. The uptide rod is generally 9–11 ft (2·7–3·3 m) long and has a reasonably rapid taper and a softish tip. This rod will cast a sinker a fair

A Shimano 'Charter Special'. A superb mid-size reel suitable for most general-purpose inshore boat fishing. It has a level wind and lever drag clutch system.

distance with only an abbreviated casting action. The tip cushions the sinker from dragging out too quickly because of the movement of the boat, as well as acting as a sensitive bite indicator.

Uptide rods do not fit easily into the IGFA system of rod classification and are generally denoted by the weight which they are intended to cast.

What is not appreciated by many anglers is that this style of rod is superb for trolling lures for bass and pollack, its extra length giving a good spread to the lures (see page 85).

Spinning rods

Under this heading I include the longer fixed-spool spinning rods and the shorter, more powerful casting rods designed for use with multiplier reels. It is probably the inshore boat angler who uses this class of rod more than anyone else. The longer – usually 8–10 ft (2·4–3 m) – carbon-fibre rods, equipped with a fixed-spool reel, are used for spinning, floatfishing, driftlining and ultra-light bottom fishing.

The 6–7 ft (1·8–2·1 m) casting rod with its trigger grip handle and mini-multiplier is used for flipping plugs, hard spinners, driftlining and light bottom fishing, particularly on extensive rocky shorelines and coves. It is an unparalleled joy to feel a good-sized bass or pollack hit a lure 10 ft (3 m) off the stern of your boat and take off on a clutch-sizzling run. I feel a charge of adrenalin just thinking about it!

REELS

Conventional boat multipliers have to be straightforward to use and rugged in their construction to take the punishing treatment dished out by the conventional 'up and down' style of conventional boat fishing.

Penn reels established the yardstick for many years with their strong, straightforward, well engineered reels. Virtually every manufacturer of boat reels copied the Penn quality and price. Many of my pals still use their Penns for much of their fishing and no doubt will continue to do so for many years to come.

In the 1980s the Japanese reel manufacturer Shimano threw down a challenge to Penn's supremacy by introducing a range of light-weight high-performance reels made from carbon-fibre and equipped with a superbly smooth lever drag, a type of clutch only seen up till that time on such expensive reels as the Penn International range. It is only recently that Penn has reacted to the challenge by making a similar reel which so far seems to be sold only in America.

There has been much discussion and argument about the star-drag versus the lever-drag system, but the consensus of informed opinion is that star-drag Penn reels with their recently introduced HT 100 clutch material are as good as you can get in a star-drag system, but that the lever-drag system has the edge, especially for light-line and line-class fishing.

Multiplier reels do not have a rating system such as the IGFA one used for rods. Instead they have a measure of size originated by Penn many years ago, whereby their reels were given a number – 6/0, for example. Ask any experienced sea angler how big, say, a Shimano TLD 25 is and he will probably reply, 'Oh, about a 6/0'.

The inshore boat angler will rarely, if ever, use a boat reel larger than a 6/0, and to give some idea of rods matched to reels, a list appears below. Note though that this list is only a guide. In practice some anglers prefer larger reels, which when well filled with line, will give a faster line retrieve. Also, because the reel is larger it will have bigger clutch washers, and the assumption is that a larger reel used lightly will last a lifetime.

IGFA Rod Rating	Penn	Shimano (TLD)
50 lb (24 kg)	6/0	25
30 lb (15 kg)	4/0	20
20 lb (10 kg)	3/0	15
16 lb (8 kg)	3/0	10
12 lb (6 kg)	2/0	5
8 lb (4 kg)	1/0	5

Of course, there are other makers of excellent reels such as ABU, Daiwa, Ryobi and Mitchell, and each angler will make his or her own choice to suit the preferred style of fishing and according to cost.

Uptide reels

Uptide reels have to perform a dual function: first they are a boat reel and second they must have some form of cast control, either centrifugal or magnetic, or a combination of both. Penn, Shimano, ABU, Daiwa and Ryobi all make reels which will perform these two tasks superbly well, but be careful when purchasing such a reel that it will resist the corrosive effects of salt water. Some reels in this class were originally intended for use in fresh water and will rot in no time. Carbon-fibre models are a safe bet.

Baitcasting reels

Baitcasting reels are basically a miniature casting multiplier, holding perhaps 150 yards (137 m) of 10 lb (4·5 kg) breaking strain monofilament line. I use mine for inshore lure fishing and shallow-water plaice and flounder fishing. On such light tackle these fish can give a good account of themselves.

Fixed-spool spinning reels

These reels have much more of a role to play on an inshore angling boat than many self-appointed experts would lead you to believe. First, spinning for mackerel, garfish, pollack or even bass can be tremendous fun and often produces surprising results. Second, float fishing with a fixed-spool reel is a versatile and excellent method of presenting a bait such as a live sandeel or prawn into places that you would be reluctant to take your boat. Third, by using the hi-tech Shimano or ABU fixed-spool reels with the 'baitrunner' facility, driftlining (see page 83) can be carried out with a degree of skill and subtlety denied by any other type of reel.

NYLON LINE

Today's nylon monofilament is soft, supple and tremendously strong for its diameter. It is available in all the IGFA line classes and a lot more breaking strains as well, to suit any requirement.

It is available in a wide variety of colours ranging from fluorescent yellow or orange through an almost invisible clear, and on through brown to solid black. There is even a multicoloured line, which I suppose is meant to act in some way as a camouflage. Over the years my personal preference has always been for line which is either clear or in the range 'light straw to brown'. The greens and blues which I suppose are meant to indicate that this is a sea line have never really appealed to my aesthetic sense.

There are a number of things to watch out for with monofilament. The slightest 'mechanical' damage such as a nick or a scratch spells trouble, because as soon as the line is put under tension it will stretch and magnify the damage beyond all proportion. The forces acting on the line will concentrate on that weak point and make it even worse.

Watch out for scored or damaged rod rings since they can spell sudden death for even brand-new line. Bad kinks and twists produced by tangling with someone else's line can also cause a weak spot in your line that from outward appearance you would never suspect. But when the line is stressed it will suddenly snap like rotten cotton.

Keep monofilament out of the sun and in a cool place if you can. The sun's ultraviolet rays can damage the line's chemical composition, while heat can leach out the plasticizer which keeps it supple. Often it is not just *one* of these damaging factors which causes your line to crack off on a good fish, but an accumulation of all of them over a period of use. If you are going on a trip where there is a chance of a good fish, don't skimp on this – renew your line and take a spare spool.

Nylon line is manufactured from various grades of nylon. Some of it is cheap and nasty (avoid 'nylon 6'), some of it dependable. The big bulk spools that you sometimes see advertised at giveaway prices are often not the bargain they might seem. First, it is probably an inferior grade of nylon; second, by the time you reach the end of the spool, it will probably have the breaking strain of chewing gum.

Don't stint on line, for it is probably the most important part of your tackle. Good makes are Maxima, especially the Silver Grade, Ande – excellent value for money – and Dupont Stren – very good line but rather expensive. The IGFA Class ABU line is very good value, and Shakespeare, Daiwa and Sylcast are good lines. Whichever you choose, renew it at regular intervals.

A 600-yard (550 m) spool of line will fill your reel twice during the season, which is about right if you fish regularly and use other rods and reels as well. If, like me, you have a couple of favourite rods which you use frequently, then it is essential to renew line at more frequent intervals, especially in the lower breaking strains.

KNOTS

I have an excellent American book that describes knots for just about every conceivable angling application. However, after much study and practical application, experience has shown me that I can do everything I want to using just two knots: the double-tucked blood knot and the uni-knot. Properly tied in top-quality monofilament these two knots will preserve over 90 per cent of the line's breaking strain.

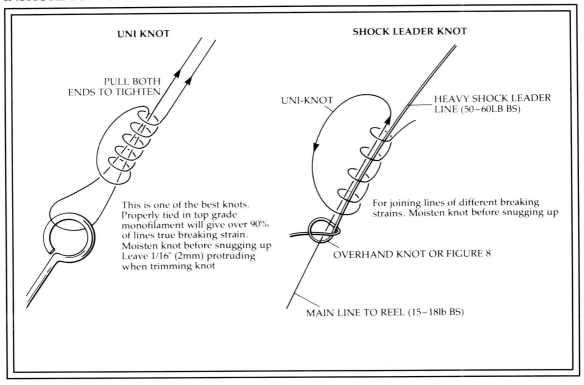

UNI KNOT

PULL BOTH
ENDS TO TIGHTEN

This is one of the best knots.
Properly tied in top grade
monofilament will give over 90%
of lines true breaking strain.
Moisten knot before snugging up
Leave 1/16" (2mm) protruding
when trimming knot

SHOCK LEADER KNOT

UNI-KNOT

HEAVY SHOCK LEADER
LINE (50–60LB BS)

For joining lines of different breaking
strains. Moisten knot before snugging up

OVERHAND KNOT OR FIGURE 8

MAIN LINE TO REEL (15–18lb BS)

Russ's Rules of Engagement – line tips

1 Choose a top-grade nylon monofilament for the greatest knot strength, longevity and resistance to abrasion.

2 ALWAYS wet monofilament before snugging the knot up. Do not overtighten. After knots have been heavily stressed and overtightened, re-tie all knots and put on a new trace.

3 If the whole of the line has seen some heavy use or has been stressed by a particularly successful trip, renew it at the earliest opportunity. The nylon molecules do not fully recover and become brittle – a sure indication of this is when the line becomes 'wirey' and hard.

4 Always use swivels, hooks and other attachments with a wire thickness greater than the line's diameter, otherwise the wire tends to cut the nylon when the line us under stress.

5 Check your trace/leader for abrasion after landing each fish, and renew it at the slightest suspicion of any scuffs or nicks.

6 Always leave a tag end of at least 1/16 in (2 mm) protruding from a knot, to allow for a degree of slippage as the knot achieves total tightness under stress.

7 Always take any gash monofilament home with you. Never discard it on the boat or dump it in the sea. I find my plastic sandwich bags make good sacks for such rubbish.

Swivels and links

It is easy to be tempted to buy a gross of cheap swivels for just a few pounds when the real thing costs two or three times as much. But it is definitely a false economy. I was only let down a couple of times by these inferior swivels before I trashed the lot, but the problem is that they look just fine. Nowadays I only use swivels that come in a maker's sealed bag, Berkley, Mustad, Drennan and Dexter all being reliable makes, and easily available.

Good-quality swivels have a remarkably high breaking strain for their size, and one of the

SNELL KNOT

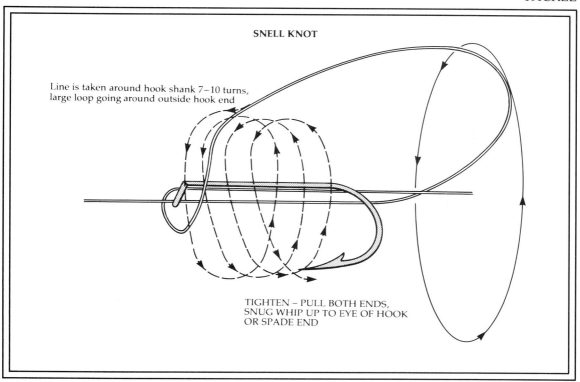

Line is taken around hook shank 7–10 turns,
large loop going around outside hook end

TIGHTEN – PULL BOTH ENDS,
SNUG WHIP UP TO EYE OF HOOK
OR SPADE END

DOUBLE TUCKED BLOOD KNOT
The best blood knot of all time!

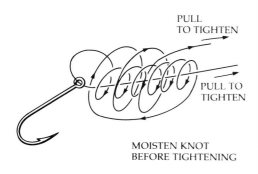

PULL
TO TIGHTEN

PULL TO
TIGHTEN

MOISTEN KNOT
BEFORE TIGHTENING

LEAVE 1/16" (2MM) OF TAG END PROTRUDING
FROM KNOT WHEN TRIMMING.
NOTE HOW TAG END WILL COME OUT
HALFWAY UP THE KNOT

problems is that if you use swivels which are too big then the line will not be stiff enough to make the swivel(s) rotate. Therefore be sure to choose a swivel size commensurate with the diameter of the line you are using.

If you find that even with a swivel in your end rig you are still getting line twist, then put another swivel or even two into your rig. Also look carefully at what is causing the line twist. Often, changing the hook from a kirbed pattern to a 'straight' hook will cure the twist. Or maybe your bait could be cut and presented better.

Link swivels can be useful in certain rigs and are a swift and convenient way of changing lures. I have lost all faith in clip links made from wire and now use only the Berkley McMahon scissor-type link, which is in my view the best you can get. The problem is obtaining the real thing in the UK, but you may find a dealer who imports them from the USA.

Crimping pliers, crimps, swivels, soft wire and hooks; for the manufacture of wire traces for conger, ling, shark and skate.

Booms

For such rigs as the long-trace 'flying collar' a stainless steel boom of 9–15 in (25–40 cm) or one of the recently introduced injection-moulded nylon booms of a similar length is necessary when fishing a Redgill or Eddystone eel in deep water. The boom gives a degree of separation between the main line and the trace as the rig sinks to the required depth, thus preventing the lure from tangling back around the main line. Shorter booms serve a similar purpose when fishing with heavier tackle for conger and ray.

The French boom is useful for fishing two different baits for such fish as bream and whiting. Its advantage is that it can easily be removed and repositioned to fish at a different depth should you find that the fish are off the bottom.

Plastic sliders

I use these a lot for bottom fishing. The red nylon zip slider is excellent. The sinker is clipped into its wire link and the line passes through the hole in the slider's plastic body. This allows the fish to pick up the bait without feeling the weight of the sinker. I use the zip slider in many situations, from plaice fishing to heavy congering, and have found it to be first class.

The white nylon sea boom fulfils a similar function, except that it will cock itself into the current rather like a wind vane.

Hooks

Your choice of hook is far more important than is immediately obvious. Think about it: the two most important items of tackle are your hook and line. Everything else is good to have, but without hook and line you cannot catch fish. This is stating the obvious, but it is amazing how many anglers will spend heavily on rods, reels, boats and everything else, yet penny-pinch on hooks and line.

Two very different steels are used in the manufacture of hooks. One is high-carbon steel, which can be hardened and tempered to make a hook which is light in weight but strong and tough for its size. It will also hold a sharp point longer than a stainless steel hook, but has the disadvantage that it is prone to rust in salt water.

Stainless steel hooks are not nearly so prone to rust or oxidize, but they can only be toughened – they cannot be hardened and tempered like high-carbon steel. Therefore a stainless hook has to be made of substantially thicker metal to possess the same strength as its carbon-steel equivalent.

In recent times the fine-wire Aberdeen-type hook has become popular. Apart from my offshore heavy fishing for shark and conger, I have to think hard to recall when I last used a hook other than an Aberdeen, in one or other of its forms. They have the advantage of being light in weight, tough, springy and needle-sharp, and as most of my inshore fishing is done with line of less than 20 lb (9 kg) breaking strain, Aberdeens suit my style perfectly.

I am not going into detail here about hook types and sizes to use. You will find this information in Chapter 6, which deals with the different species.

Hints on hooks

1   Hooks are not expensive, so buy the best.

2   When buying small quantities of hooks over the counter, be a nuisance: examine each one visually. Check that:

• the eye is closed tight, free from burrs and sharp edges.

• the point is nicely formed and smooth right up to the barb.

• the barb is not cut too deeply into the wire.

• the shank and bend are smooth, nicely formed and free from tool marks.

• the plating is even all over and free from any surface irregularities.

3   Don't take too many hooks on a trip – just enough. Leave the rest home in the dry.

4   Keep hooks sharp. Carry and use a sharpening stone or better still a purpose-made diamond file. Sharpen large hooks such as the Mustad Sea Masters with a fine file and bring them to final sharpness with the sharpening stone.

5   As with all tackle, 'If in doubt, chuck it out!' The fish of a lifetime rarely comes back for a second bite.

SINKERS

It is a long time since I bought any sinkers, I much prefer to make my own. Sinker shapes are largely a matter of personal preference. My view is that rounded sinkers are better in most instances than those with flat surfaces. But I am a firm believer in letting local conditions and individual preference determine what is best on a given patch.

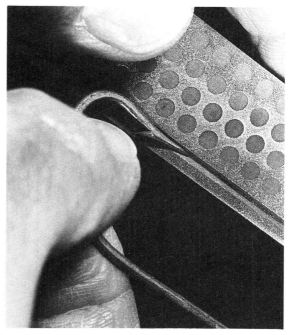

It is important that hooks are kept needle sharp. This hook is being sharpened using a special diamond-impregnated file. These files never rust and seem to last for ever. They are expensive, but I have been using this one for over 10 years.

DIY sinkers

Fitting sinker moulds with a hinge and handles makes the production sequence quicker and a lot safer. So when purchasing moulds, make sure there is enough metal around them to fasten the hinge and handles, or else you will have to work with heavy leather gloves and a vice.

To melt the lead I use a portable gas stove, which soon warms up my garage when I have a sinker-making session of a winter's afternoon. An old-fashioned cast-iron saucepan with a pronounced pouring lip will make a superb smelting pot, particularly if it has an insulated handle.

Molten lead is dangerous and should be treated with great respect. So when making sinkers follow these simple safety rules.

- Work in a well-ventilated area – a garage or garden shed with the door open is ideal.
- Always wear a face mask or at least safety goggles. Wear gloves and cover all bare skin.
- Ensure that your moulds are warm and dry before pouring lead into them.
- Get the lead really hot, and pour it in a continuous stream. A concertina texture on the surface of the sinker indicates that the mould is not hot enough.
- Cut the lead into small pieces, so that when put in the pot it will soon melt. Remove any paint or grease from the lead before melting it, otherwise it will give off noxious fumes.
- Make sinker loops from brass or copper wire so that sinkers left aboard your boat will still have a usable loop after a season or two in the salty atmosphere.
- Take care. Do not rush. Be safe, not sorry.

GAFFS AND LANDING NETS

Getting a fish aboard your boat after playing it to a standstill should be no great problem, but it is a fact that most fish are lost in the first few seconds after the strike or in the last few seconds before being landed.

A good gaff and landing net are essential equipment for small boat angling. I usually make my own. This presents little difficulty as Mustad sell excellent gaff hooks which your dealer can order for you from their catalogue. Whip the hook to a straight-grained, stout broom handle, and you have a superbly serviceable gaff.

Landing net rims can also be bought and fitted with a net and handle for half the cost of the shop-bought item.

Whether you choose to use the gaff or the net will depend on your judgement at the time, but remember: bring the fish to the gaff or net, and

Lead sinkers are becoming increasingly expensive, especially in the larger sizes. Making your own is not difficult, providing you have a good mould and observe precautions to ensure your own safety. Fitting the mould with a hinge and insulated handles aids safe handling of the molten metal, as well as increasing the speed of manufacture.

avoid stabbing at it or you will knock it off the hook. The fish comes to the surface, is carefully drawn over the net and lifted out. It sounds simple and it is. Only the inexperienced make it complicated.

Much the same technique is used in gaffing. Draw the fish's head towards the gaff and bring the point up through its lower jaw. You are then in control and will not have damaged the vital organs, should you decide to return the fish to the sea. Gaffing the fish through the body usually drives the fish into a frenzy and can spoil it for eating as well.

Last Rites
Killing fish that you intend to take home to eat should be done quickly and efficiently. Letting a fish flap around on the deck while it dies is cruel and unsportsmanlike. A short weighted club known as a priest is the traditional instrument used to dispatch trout and salmon, and many sea anglers use them to kill sea fish. Even a metal bar serves exactly the same purpose.

It is very easy on a good day at sea to kill fish that you don't need. But if fish are being killed for no purpose, then the morality of it is for you to judge. I like to think that all true anglers will catch what they want, then try to another species or move to a different mark. A plastic bag full of dead fish thrown onto the dock is not the sign of a good angler – at least not in my book.

Unhooking
Over the years there have been some ingenious inventions intended to remove hooks from the mouths of fish. Most of these contraptions are useless, however, and are more successful at removing money from the pockets of anglers than they are at removing hooks.

If you ever get the opportunity to go to sea aboard a commercial longliner, do so. It is an experience you will never forget. The fisherman on such a vessel might have to remove his hooks from hundreds of fish in a day. For larger

fish he will use a 'jumper' and for smaller fish and smaller hooks a 'swizel stick'.

The jumper is a metal rod with a hook at one end after the fashion of a crochet hook. One hand grasps the line and the jumper hook engages in the bend of the hook. By pulling down on the line and lifting with the jumper, the hook is inverted, and then with a brisk shake the fish's own weight pulls the hook free.

The swizel stick is no more than a length of broom handle turned to a long tapered point. One hand grasps the line, lifting the fish. Then the point of the swizel stick is put as close to the hook as possible and the fish is swung around the swizel stick until the line is wrapped around the stick right up to the hook. The momentum of the fish swinging around the stick disgorges the hook as if by magic, even if the hook is a long way down inside the fish.

So before you spend good money on fancy 'gizmo's', try the jumper and the swizel stick – you won't be disappointed.

An Angler's Knife
I sometimes shudder as I watch anglers on a charter boat using lethal, long-bladed filleting knives for simple tasks such as cutting line. A simple pair of electrician's side-cut snips is far better for this task and will easily cut line of up to 300 lb (135 kg) breaking strain. They can then be shoved in your pocket without fear of injury.

Filleting knives are excellent for filleting flatfish such as plaice and flounder, but if ever you watch a professional fillet a fish it is likely that he or she will do the job with a blade hardly longer than a pocket knife. For the last ten years I have carried a heavy-duty pocket knife, a Big Swede, in a leather pouch on my belt. It has done everything from filleting flats to chunking up cod steaks. My personal opinion is that long-bladed filleting knives are not what they are cracked up to be and are posey rather than practical.

CHAPTER FIVE

TECHNIQUES

INSIDE INFORMATION

Hi-tech tackle is nice to own and use, but tackle does not catch fish – it only lands them. The inshore boat angler's most important piece of tackle is not his rods and reels, but his boat, and the knowledge and knowhow that goes with it.

As anglers we make a conscious decision to catch fish for sport, pitting our wits against the last of this planet's truly wild creatures. Catching fish is all about putting yourself in the right place at the right time and then presenting the right bait or lure in a manner which is attractive to them.

It is amazing how fish follow patterns of behaviour which are subtly altered by weather and tides. These are facts keenly appreciated by professional fishermen who, perhaps because they work at catching fish every day, intuitively follow the seasons, without thinking, altering location and technique to maximize their catch. Anglers do not have this continuity of individual experience, so we do the best we can by remembering and recording when, where and how we caught fish. In this way we gradually accumulate an armoury of techniques for fishing for different species in different conditions. These techniques are the subject of this chapter.

The sea angling grapevine carries a lot of useful information, but it also carries more than its share of 'disinformation', to deceive the inexperienced. If you suspect that another boat had a good catch miles away from where they said, then watch for them when the same tide occurs a fortnight hence, and go and have a look to confirm your suspicions. Most times if you are right, you will be greeted with a wry smile and a friendly wave, maybe even some shouted advice. The VHF will be out of bounds, especially if bass are involved. The professionals are very good at triangulating your position from VHF transmissions: one reason for having CB or even 2-metre band radios on angling boats.

LEDGERING

Ledgering is a method with an infinite variety of applications, and in one form or another it will catch just about every species of fish that swims around our shores.

Heavy ledger

The heavy ledger is generally used for the larger bottom-feeding species such as conger, ling and skate. Its intention is to anchor a large bait to the sea bed where the fish can be expected to find it. This is a static form of angling in which the boat is anchored or on the slowest of drifts. When the fish show signs of activity the rod is held, and during the waiting time the rod can be propped against the gunnel or held in a rod rest, and a watchful eye kept on it.

The sinker is generally from 12 oz (340 gm) up to 2 lb (0·9 kg) if the tide is fierce. The sinker is clipped to a zip slider or a white nylon sea boom. The old-fashioned wire Kilmore and Clements booms seem to have given way to the cheaper and better plastic booms. The main line of 30 lb (14 kg) breaking strain or more is threaded through the slider or boom and a swivel is tied to the end of the line. From this swivel runs the trace of 2–6 ft (0·6–1·8 m) in length, which can be wire or heavy-duty commercial monofilament of 100 lb (45 kg) or more breaking strain, depending on the species sought. Large 8/0 and 12/0 hooks are used, often Mustad Sea Master or Sea Demon pattern, again depending on the species.

The line can slide through the boom as the fish picks up the bait, and if you allow a little slack line in the initial stages of the bite, the fish can pick up the bait and start to move away without feeling the weight of the sinker. If the fish are in a feeding frenzy and hit the bait as if there was no tomorrow, then the boom holding the sinker is best fastened with a thick elastic band tied to the main line. This will present less of a danger to the person gaffing the fish, especially if there are several fish on the surface at once, waiting for the gaff. A clout on the head from a heavy sinker is not conducive to shipboard harmony.

Medium ledger

This is a scaled-down version of the heavy ledger, using sinkers of 4–12 oz (110–340 gm). This rig is generally used for reef conger, ling and cod, and over more open ground for ray, plaice, haddock, turbot and tope. The same slider or boom and rig set-up as for the heavy ledger is used. The trace is often longer, depending on the species, with maybe another swivel 2–3 ft (0·6–0·9 m) from the hook. This swivel is often three-way, with an additional shorter hook length especially for flatfish.

Light ledger

Often this is a simple set-up consisting of a pierced ball weight threaded onto the main line, then a soft plastic bead to protect the knot, then the main line tied to a swivel. The trace from this swivel can be anything up to 20 ft (6 m) in length, especially when the bait is live sandeel. Usually another small swivel is in-

A 62-lb conger eel. The conger eel has always been a prime target for the inshore boat angler. A thick, wet sack over the conger's head will often quieten the eel for those few vital moments while you get the fish boxes organized.

cluded in the trace 2–3 ft (0·6–0·9 m) from the hook.

The light ledger is probably the inshore boat angler's main method. I often use this rig with 10 lb (4·5 kg) line for bream, whiting, plaice, pollack, bass and flounder. I change the size of the sinker to cope with the changing tidal conditions and maybe modify the length of my trace according to the species sought.

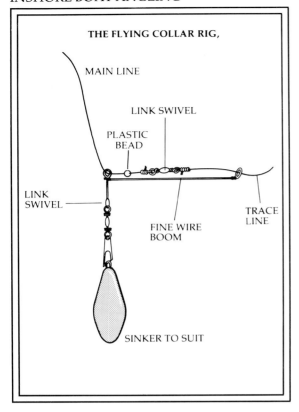

THE FLYING COLLAR RIG,

MAIN LINE

LINK SWIVEL

PLASTIC BEAD

LINK SWIVEL

FINE WIRE BOOM

TRACE LINE

SINKER TO SUIT

The flying collar

This variation of the light ledger is basically a rig which uses a long, flowing trace. It originated many years ago as a sporting method of catching the hard-fighting pollack from the rocks and canyons of the West Country reefs such as the Eddystone and Hands Deeps.

The traditional and in my view the best rig, consists of a fine springy stainless steel boom which allows the line to pass through its top two eyes and the sinker to be suspended from its downward leg. These booms can be purchased or home made from stainless wire, and the length of the top leg can vary from 9 in (23 cm) up to 15–16 in (38–41 cm). I have always found the 9 in (23 cm) commercially available booms very adequate.

There are several variations on the method of rigging the boom, the simplest of which is the one generally used for wreck fishing for deep-water pollack and coalfish, with the boom fixed. The main line is clipped to the boom using a link swivel and the trace clipped to the other end of the boom with another link swivel. The trace length in deep water is about 10 ft (3 m) but up to 15 ft (4·5 m) in a slack tide. Another swivel is usually included 2–3 ft (0·6–0·9 m) from the hook, and the short length of line from this swivel is usually of a heavier gauge – say 20 lb (9 kg) breaking strain at the minimum. Watch this hook length carefully, as the abrasive jaws of the pollack and coalfish will soon weaken it.

My favourite method of rigging this boom is to pass my main line through the first eye of the boom, through a soft plastic bead and then tie it off to a small swivel. From the other end of this swivel tie your trace line about 12 ft (3·5 m) long, with another swivel 2–3 ft (0·6–0·9 m) from the hook. This method is the one favoured for reef fishing with mackerel strip and worm baits. Plastic sandeels such as the Eddystone or Redgill also work well, as do the American Mr Twister-type lures.

The fixed-boom wreck method is used almost exclusively with plastic sandeels, but if bream are on the wreck, then bait such as mackerel strip can be used on the same rig very effectively.

If you decide to use bait, be careful that it does not spin as it sinks, otherwise your trace will end up as a ball of monofilament around your boom. Many anglers shorten the trace to 5–6 ft (1·5–1·8 m) when bait-fishing for bream.

To fish this long-trace method, the lure or bait is allowed to stream away in the tide, then the boom and sinker are gently flipped away up-tide, to ensure the maximum separation between boom and lure (bait) before the descent into the depths begins. Lower away gently, your thumb regulating the spool speed so that the boom can do its job of keeping the trace and main line separated. As soon as you feel the sinker just tap the bottom, commence your retrieve, slowly in a fast tide and quite quickly in a slack tide.

See how far up in the water the fish are from your echo-sounder, and count up the number of turns on your reel to reach this depth. This is often a subjective judgement based on the retrieve ratio of the reel you are using, the angle at which the tide is streaming your tackle, and honest, hard-won experience. If you are fishing for pollack and coalfish and you feel the fish pluck at your lure, do not stop reeling or the fish will lose interest. Keep on winding, and most often the next thing you will feel will be the tip of your rod dipping towards the sea under the weight of the fish, as it starts its Kamikaze dive for freedom.

It is at this point that most fish are lost, as the ignorant or inexperienced angler tries to stop this power-dive. This is the moment of truth for cheap tackle, last year's line and poorly tied knots. If you are prepared and the reel's clutch is pre-set at about half the line's breaking strain, then you have got a chance if the fish is a good one. If you haven't got it together, be sure to learn from the experience!

FREELINING/DRIFTLINING
This is possibly the simplest of all sea angling techniques, yet it is in this utter simplicity that its subtlety lies. Used with perception and skill, freelining is the most deadly of methods.

The rig is no more than a hook tied to the end of your line, usually a fine-wire Aberdeen for lightness. A sandeel is lightly nicked to the hook and allowed to swim away in the tide. Often 50–60 yards (46–55 m) of line are allowed to peel off before the spool is stopped. There are differences of opinion as to whether it is best at this point to set your reel on the ratchet or put it into gear on a light clutch setting. I don't think it matters that much, because when a fish picks up the bait it is such a natural presentation that the fish will usually gulp it down anyway before it realizes that the angler is being craftier than usual.

Freelining, then, can be seen as a simple method, but it is deciding when and where to use it that makes demands on the angler's ex-

perience and appreciation of conditions, species, bait-fish and other variables. He must know when to go to anchor and present a bait over a known reef or confluence of currents, distancing boat and noise from the fish. This is a method for those quiet times inshore, when the pleasure of using forethought, skill and subtlety in pursuit of one or two good fish outweighs the attraction of fishing to fill the freezer.

FLOATFISHING
What is the point of floatfishing from a boat, many of you will ask. To fish inshore from a boat in the West Country is to haunt the coves and reefs which reach out from this wild and rock-strewn shoreline, and most of us will venture into some 'skinny' water when the tides are high and conditions are flat. Usually we have to anchor off and driftline or floatfish a bait in over those areas of wild sanctuary, taking our chances on being able to fight the fish out of the cover. It is useful to be able to cast your float rig 40–50 yards (37–46 m) if the occasion warrants it. So the rig which is universally used is what is known as a sliding float rig.

The float can be up to 1 ft (30 cm) long by maybe 1 in (2·5 cm) in diameter and made from polystyrene painted black on the bottom and fluorescent orange or yellow on the top. Generally my ideal float is 6–7 in (15–18 cm) long by about ½ in (1 cm) in diameter. This will carry a ½-oz (15 gm) sinker and is easily the best size to use for pollack, bass and mackerel. The float is rigged by first sliding a soft plastic bead onto the main line, and the line is then passed through the plastic tube, which passes through the length of the float. Sinkers can be a pierced ball or an egg sinker which is slipped onto the line, followed by another soft plastic bead, before the line is tied off at a swivel. From this swivel the trace is tied, maybe up to 4–5 ft (1·2–1·5 m) long but normally about 3 ft (0·9 m).

The depth at which your bait will fish is now set by tying with a series of hitches a small length of rubber band or, better still, elasticated cotton, onto the main line above the bead/float.

What happens is that if you set the bait depth at, say, 20 ft (6 m) and then cast out, the sinker will hit the water and go down, taking the baited hook and pulling your main line through the float. When the little knot of elastic reaches the bead on top of the float the bait depth will be set, and the float will settle and start to fish.

The best tackle for this method is 9–10 ft (2·7–3 m) carbon-fibre spinning rod equipped with a small to medium-sized fixed-spool reel. I generally use monofilament of about 10 lb (4·5 kg) breaking strain, which I often grease with fly-line grease so that the line does not sink and delay the strike.

There is something mesmeric about watching a float, keyed up and waiting to give the instantaneous wind and strike which will drive the hook home.

SPINNING

Casting a metal lure, a leadhead jig with an American-style plastic worm, or casting a floating or sinking plug, is a small boat method much underrated in British waters. Good fish like bass and pollack are often much closer inshore than many anglers believe. These fish live by eating sandeels and brit, which I believe to be their preferred diet, and there are few thrills in sea angling to match that heart-tripping moment when some unseen predator smashes into a plastic plug.

Anglers in small boats are in a privileged position to enjoy this superb sport, but it takes some thought, imagination and single-minded persistence to exploit it. If you know, for instance, that bass are regularly caught at a particular point, then anchoring or drifting that spot

Plug fishing for bass and pollack has proven to be a deadly method when the fish are feeding. It also provides the angler with an exciting and superbly visual method of catching these predatory fish.

during the quiet hours of dawn or dusk working a plug such as the Rapala Sliver or Yo-Zuri Shad may well produce fish that your wildest imagination could hardly conjure up. I have been amazed on more than a few occasions to catch fish only yards from the shore, and yet when I relate the story it never fails to meet with scepticism.

Because this style of fishing is not a mainstream activity in the UK, tackle to do it properly is difficult to find. Reels, though, are not much of a problem: the Shimano Bantamlite multipliers and the ABU XLT Synchro are both reels I use myself and recommend. Fixed-spool reels have to be of top quality to withstand the rough and tumble of this type of fishing. The Shimano Biomaster GT 3000 is my favourite, with the Aero 3000 and ABU Cardinals close behind. Rods are a problem because I like a short rod rather than the longer rod which seems to be preferred in UK waters. A consequence of this is that I have ended up making my own from light beachcaster tips. Among the longer rods the specialist 10 ft (3 m) Tekno Bass Spinner is the specialist tool for this job, and is equally useful for floatfishing.

This method of fishing undoubtedly has a great future as more anglers discover its thrills and skills.

TROLLING

Trolling, or whiffing as it is known in the West Country, is a method which remains a mystery to most anglers. Probably the main reason for this is that it is the method favoured by the professional bass fishermen, and they are very tight-lipped when it comes to when, where and how to catch bass.

I know of no method which will catch so many bass as whiffing will on a good day – and on bad days everyone struggles, no matter what method they use. Tackle does not mean a thing with this method. Indeed, one of the men I learnt from could get a bass in and the lure back out again twice as fast with a handline as I could with the very best of rods and reels. Experience and an intelligent appreciation of what the fish are doing is everything.

Trolling is a method where a lure is trailed 60–80 yards (55–75 m) behind your boat, in depths of water and places where bass are known to shoal at certain stages of the tide. This is the information that you will have to work very hard to find out. You will be fed 'disinformation', deceived and told downright lies by people you thought you could trust. They will only work certain spots at dawn and dusk, even though the fish will be there and feeding during the day. Believe me, they are a secretive lot!

Anyway, here is the method. The rest is up to you. Your boat must be capable of prolonged slow speeds. The best type for trolling is a wooden boat with a quiet, slow-running diesel engine. The problem most of us will face is that our outboard-powered boats are just too fast if we use our main engines, and two-stroke outboards do not take kindly to extended running at tick-over speeds: the plugs oil up and cause all sorts of problems. Today's generation of two-strokes with computer-controlled oil/petrol mix – so that at tick-over, the oil/petrol mix could be down to 200–1 or thereabouts – are far better equipped to cope with extended low-speed running than are the traditional two-stroke outboards.

Mariner Outboards have produced a range of outboards of between 6 and 15 horsepower in which the oil/petrol mix and tick-over speed can be adjusted manually from a fascia-mounted control on the engine – especially for trolling. These Mariner engines are a direct response to the threat to their trolling outboard market posed by Honda's four-stroke engines, which can work all day at slow speeds with no detrimental effect.

What many anglers are doing is using a big engine for moving about at speed and a trolling motor for slow-speed work and as a 'get you home' reserve engine – an eminently sensible arrangement.

Professional bass trollers will often use outriggers – either custom-made fibreglass poles imported from the USA or, as is more usual, 12–15 ft (3·5–4·5 m) bamboo canes tapering from about a diameter of about 2 in (5 cm) down to 1 in (2·5 cm), with the top section made from an old 50-lb (24 kg) class rod tip. Most anglers, however, spread their lures by putting their rods in tubular rod holders, so that most of the rod protrudes over the side of the boat. Ten-foot (3 m) uptide boat rods make favourite trolling rods: the lures are then separated by the beam of the boat, plus another 16 ft (5 m) from the two rods.

The reel's clutch and ratchet are set just hard enough to put a heavy set in the rod when a fish strikes. This will generally set the hook, but when you pick up the rod the first thing to do is wind in furiously until you feel the weight of the fish, then give a heavy strike – just to make sure.

Eddystone Eels and Redgills are the favourite lures: the pearl with blue or green backs have proven to be the most deadly colour combinations. It is important that the lure 'swims' in an upright position. If it lies on its side as the boat moves along, then the hook position in the lure's body cavity has to be altered until the lure swims properly.

The size of sinker used will largely depend on how high the bass are in the water. If you can see the gulls working, picking up the remains of unfortunate sandeels, then the bass are high in the water, and the amount of lead should vary from nothing at all (the gulls can be a pest) to ½ oz (15 gm). Bass caught on the top like this will rarely weigh over 5 lb (2·5 kg) – these are young fast fish.

Going from ½ oz (15 gm) to 2 oz (60 gm) will take your lures down to about 25 ft (7·5 m), depending on how fast you troll. The deep fish are the larger ones. The amount of line you put out is usually measured by the number of 'pulls' – each about a yard (0·9 m).

Monofilament line of about 15–18 lb (7–8 kg) breaking strain is generally used. The trace from the lure to the swivel (I use ball-bearing swivels) is usually 5–6 ft (1·5–2 m), so that the

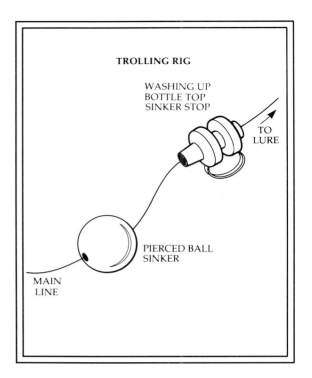

TROLLING RIG

WASHING UP BOTTLE TOP SINKER STOP

TO LURE

PIERCED BALL SINKER

MAIN LINE

fish can be easily played to the net. Above the swivel you thread on first a pierced ball or egg sinker, then the plastic top from a liquid detergent bottle. After you have ensured that your lure is swimming properly, hold the sinker and bottle top in your hand and make 20 pulls, and then snap the bottle top shut – this will grip your line and keep your sinker in position.

Make another 50 pulls, set the reel's clutch and put the rod in its holder. This should be done with the boat under way. Your fishing companion will have done the same to the other rod. Do not use the same weight of sinker on both rods, otherwise no matter how gently you make a turn, a tangle will result.

Uptide Casting

This is a method of bottom fishing which has much to commend it in shallow water, especially if there are just one or two of you on board. Basically it consists of going to anchor, then casting your baited hook some 50 yards (46 m) uptide and away from the boat.

The anchor rope will 'drum' in the current,

Conservation is more than a word to most committed anglers. Fish that are not required are usually returned. Allan Paddon returns a fine coalfish while a recent landing ban was in force.

There area number of excellent uptide rods made by Daiwa, Normark, Conoflex and others. Reels are standard beachcasting reels, but the Shimano TSM 2CFS could have been specifically made for 'uptiding', so perfectly does it fit the purpose.

The line is normally 15–18 lb (7–8 kg) breaking strain monofilament. My usual rig is very simple: just a 5-oz (140 gm) long-tailed breakaway sinker with a three-way swivel 3 ft (0·9 m) up from the sinker, then a 3-ft (0·9 m) leader from the third eye of the swivel.

After casting allow some slack line so that the sinker finds the bottom and grips. Then gently pick up some of the slack until you have a comfortable curve in the rod tip yet enough line out so that the action of the waves does not trip the sinker.

Bites are usually signalled by the line going slack as the fish trips the sinker and the rod tip nodding to the bite. Pick the rod up, point the tip down the line and reel in quickly until you feel the weight of the fish. Then lift the rod into the weight of the fish, which will set the hook with certainty.

Sometimes the bite is just a straightening of the line as a fish picks up the bait, realizes that all is not what it seems and takes off at speed. It is very important that you have your reel's clutch set just hard enough to prevent line from peeling off under the pressure of the current. I then engage the ratchet to give me an audible indication of a bite. In this way you will not lose your rod and reel to a hard and unexpected bite. I often use an elastic bungee to secure my rod against the unexpected.

there will be inevitable boat noise and as sound travels six times faster in water than it does in air, the fish, being wild creatures, will make a detour around the source of the sound. With luck there will be more fish in the vicinity of your bait than will pass close to the boat. The results certainly speak for themselves.

CHAPTER SIX

THE FISH

BASS

The bass is Britain's finest saltwater sport fish. Not only is it the most handsome of fish with its silver scales and well-proportioned shape, but it is arguably the roughest, toughest fighting fish that swims around our shores, when caught on sporting tackle.

It is not only how they fight which makes bass such a hard-won prize, but also how they feed, because they can be caught, in the right circumstances, by every method in the book: ledgering, floatfishing, spinning, flyfishing, plugging, driftlining, trolling, uptide or downtide. Choose the tide, time and place, and if you are skilful and persistent enough you will catch your bass.

Bass are ultrasensitive to noise and disturbance, and will skirt boat noise by a fair margin, only coming close to a boat to attack a lure, which they may well have followed for many yards. When I fish uptide or at anchor for bass, I take great care to keep as quiet as possible and avoid starting engines if I am anywhere near the shoal.

For many anglers the bass has an addictive quality, due in no small part to the often wild and beautiful places which this marvellous fish prefers as its habitat. Then just to add that contradictory element which gives an edge to the fascination, bass can be caught close inshore in the most densely populated areas such as harbours and marinas, usually after dark, as they hunt the prawns, baby pout and sandeels which frequent these areas.

The bass is a fish governed by a strict minimum-size limit of 36 cm (14 in). Most anglers voluntarily return any bass that is under about 18 in (46 cm) and indeed if you do not need the fish put them back irrespective of size. Bass are very slow-growing and they are under enough commercial pressure without anglers adding unnecessarily to their problems.

A good bass is played to the side of the boat, ready for the landing net; a sight to gladden the heart of any angler.

Tackle

Since there is such a wide range of methods which can be used to catch bass, tackle will vary to a large extent according to the method employed. Generally, however, tackle should not be heavier than a 20 lb (10 kg) class conventional outfit, or a 5 oz (140 gm) casting-weight uptide rod.

Method

In shallow water up to, say, 50 ft (15 m), uptide casting from an anchored boat is an excellent method. Use a running ledger consisting of a zip slider on your shock leader, the slider stopped with a bead and swivel, and from the other side of the swivel a trace of 3–5 ft (1–1·5 m). If just one or two of you are fishing, the ideal size of sinker is just enough weight to hold bottom, or a light breakaway sinker.

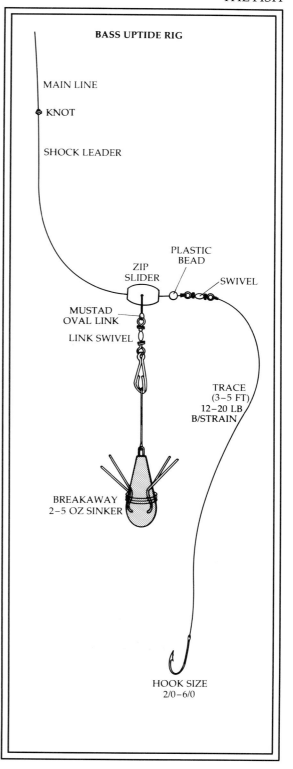

BASS UPTIDE RIG

MAIN LINE

KNOT

SHOCK LEADER

PLASTIC BEAD

ZIP SLIDER

SWIVEL

MUSTAD OVAL LINK

LINK SWIVEL

TRACE (3–5 FT) 12–20 LB B/STRAIN

BREAKAWAY 2–5 OZ SINKER

HOOK SIZE 2/0–6/0

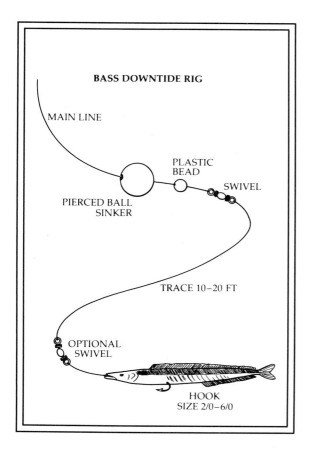

BASS DOWNTIDE RIG

MAIN LINE

PLASTIC BEAD

SWIVEL

PIERCED BALL SINKER

TRACE 10–20 FT

OPTIONAL SWIVEL

HOOK SIZE 2/0–6/0

Although uptide casting has proven itself time and again to be the most productive method from an anchored boat, many anglers still prefer to fish downtide, as I do myself occasionally. Use a 12 lb (6 kg) or 16 lb (8 kg) class outfit for best sport and a simple running ledger consisting of a pierced ball or egg sinker threaded onto your main line and stopped by a bead and swivel. From the other side of this swivel, long traces of up to 20 ft (6 m) can be employed, especially when using live sandeel bait.

From a drifting boat an identical rig is used except that the trace is normally shorter at about 10 ft (3 m). Also when on the drift, lighter tackle – 8–10 lb (3·5–4·5 kg) line, say – can be used, because you will not be fighting the tide as well as the fish.

Driftlining is conventional downtide fishing usually from an anchored boat, without the sinker, or with the very least you can use, often just a split shot, and this only to take your prawn or sandeel down out of the reach of diving seagulls.

Bass often shoal near the surface to prey on the schools of brit or sandeel and driftlining an eel back to the bass is a painstaking but deadly method of catching them.

Floatfishing

Floatfishing shares many of the advantages of driftlining, but has the bonus that you can cast float gear 50–60 yards (46–55 m) when the wind is behind you. This then allows your bait to float into the fish-holding area without the disturbance of boat and engine noise. It also allows you to fish in areas into which you may be reluctant to take your boat.

The sliding float rig consists of a float with a central tube through which your line passes. Thread onto your main line a soft plastic bead, the float, a pierced ball or egg sinker heavy enough to cock the float leaving about one third of its length showing, then a plastic bead, and tie off the main line to a good-quality swivel. From the other side of the swivel tie a 3–5 ft

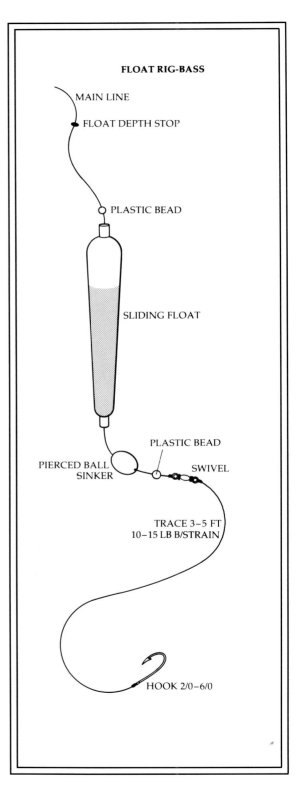

FLOAT RIG-BASS

MAIN LINE

FLOAT DEPTH STOP

PLASTIC BEAD

SLIDING FLOAT

PLASTIC BEAD

PIERCED BALL SINKER

SWIVEL

TRACE 3–5 FT
10–15 LB B/STRAIN

HOOK 2/0–6/0

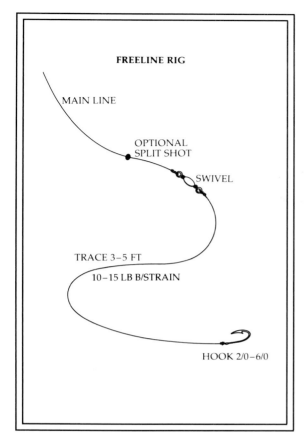

FREELINE RIG

MAIN LINE

OPTIONAL
SPLIT SHOT

SWIVEL

TRACE 3–5 FT

10–15 LB B/STRAIN

HOOK 2/0–6/0

(1–1·5 m) trace. The depth at which your bait will fish can then be set by tying a small rubber band, or even better a short length of elasticated cotton, to your main line above the bead and float. A two-handed spinning rod and fixed-spool reel such as the Shimano Baitrunner is the ideal tackle for freelining and floatfishing.

Spinning and plugfishing

I regard spinning for bass as using hard metal lures such as the classic ABU Toby and the American leadhead lures. Plugfishing is also spinning of a sort, but this method is far more deadly than many anglers realize. Such lures as the Rapala Sliver and Shad Rap, and Yo-Zuri plugs worked from a drifting boat provide an exciting and productive way of catching bass, but you have to be sure that you know where the fish are.

Trolling

Trolling as described on page 85 can be an excellent technique for catching bass, and indeed is practised by many professional fishermen. It bears repeating, however, that your lure must 'swim' properly or you will frighten more bass than you will catch.

Lures

The best lures include pearl Eddystone Eels with black or blue backs, and Redgills. Rapala Sliver and Silver Shad plugs and the Yo-Zuri plugs are also excellent. The ABU Killer Balsa is almost identical to the Rapala Original and is a standard bass plug of the highest order.

Among metal spinners the original Norwegian Tobys, the ABU Toby and now unfortunately extinct Krill, or the Krill copy which can be found in some tackle shops, are recommended. The rough-looking Yann lures of French origin are also excellent on their day.

Leadheads and Plastic worms

Leadheads are a much underestimated type of lure, and I have caught many fish on this sort of lure. Worked 'sink and draw' over rock and weed they certainly catch bass and pollack. Mr Twister Leadheads are in particular to be recommended.

Baits

Live and, occasionally, frozen sandeel, peeler crab, prawn, lugworm, king ragworm, squid and mackerel.

Hooks

Recommended are Mustad Aberdeens, Mustad 79515, Cox and Rawle Real Tackle uptide, Kamasan – in sizes 2/0–6/0.

BREAM

Two types of bream are fairly common in British waters, the Red bream and the Black bream. They inhabit the same sort of ground and will take the same baits. Some say the black fights harder than the red, but I do not agree. I think they are both fine sporting fish.

Both varieties of bream show their strength and stamina on light tackle, and as the heaviest fish that you might ever encounter might just make double figures, give yourself a thrill by fishing light.

Tackle

The tackle and methods are the same for both species: 8 lb (4 kg) or 12 lb (6 kg) class outfits are ideal. If you do not own such light tackle, then your inshore spinning outfit loaded with 10 lb (4·5 kg) line will serve you well.

Method

A fine-wire boom, flying-collar rig with a 6 ft (1·8 m) trace is ideal in deep water. In shallow water a pierced bullet or egg sinker threaded onto your main line, stopped at the swivel by a soft plastic bead, with a 6 ft (1·8 m) trace from the swivel is the perfect rig.

Often bream can be found tucked right into the leeward side of a wreck or reef. In slack water they will spread out over top of it, forag-ing for feed. Late in the evening they will come right up in the water, and I have actually seen bream take my bait just a few feet down. Some rubby-dubby or Chum chunks fed slowly to them will keep their interest. Fishing for them by freelining a small bait on ultra-light tackle is truly supreme sport.

Baits

King ragworm cocktailed with a small mackerel or squid strip has caught me a lot of bream over the years, but mackerel strip on its own is a good bait.

Hooks

Fine-wire Aberdeens in sizes 1/0 or 2/0 are ideal. A quick, sharp strike is necessary, or the bream will strip the bait from the hook in an instant. This results in a high proportion of lip-hooked fish, which are easily shaken off. (Bream are a fine table fish and so have been commercially hammered. Therefore bream which you do not want for the table should be shaken off in the water, if you can.)

Red bream are a fish which unfortunately have become more difficult to find in the past few years, largely because of commercial overfishing in the nursery areas. They are a fine sporting fish on light tackle and a real prize for the table.

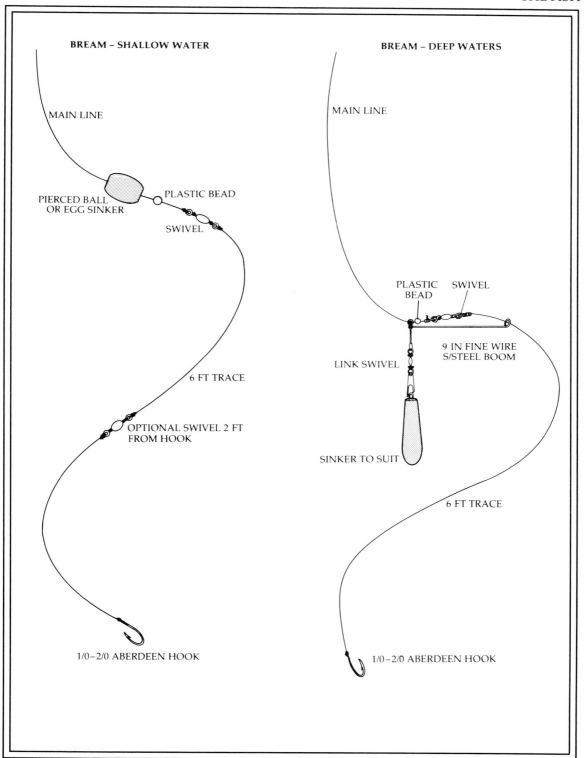

BREAM – SHALLOW WATER

MAIN LINE

PIERCED BALL
OR EGG SINKER

PLASTIC BEAD

SWIVEL

6 FT TRACE

OPTIONAL SWIVEL 2 FT
FROM HOOK

1/0–2/0 ABERDEEN HOOK

BREAM – DEEP WATERS

MAIN LINE

PLASTIC
BEAD

SWIVEL

9 IN FINE WIRE
S/STEEL BOOM

LINK SWIVEL

SINKER TO SUIT

6 FT TRACE

1/0–2/0 ABERDEEN HOOK

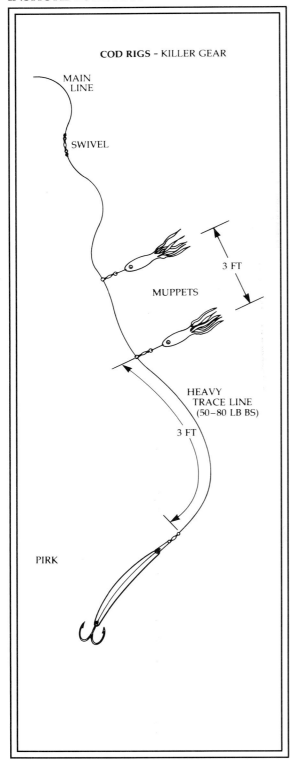

COD RIGS - KILLER GEAR

MAIN
LINE

SWIVEL

3 FT

MUPPETS

HEAVY
TRACE LINE
(50–80 LB BS)

3 FT

PIRK

COD

The cod is Britain's most widely distributed and popular sea fish. It bites well, thumps its tail a few times and tastes good. A lovely-looking fish when fresh from the sea, it is also pleasing to catch. When cod come on the feed they are not difficult to catch, whether over a deep water wreck or even uptide fishing in shallow estuarial waters.

Almost all my fishing is done out of my home port of Plymouth, and although we catch a fair number of cod, our methods and seasons are different from those of most other parts of Britain. This is probably true wherever you live, and regional differences in seasons and methods have to be learnt by experience on your own patch, especially for cod.

The basic uptide and conventional downtide methods described below are no more than a starting point, and it will pay you to watch other anglers who are more successful than the average. Sometimes just a minor change in tackle or technique can make all the difference between consistent success and abysmal failure.

Although cod are caught out on the deepwater wrecks all year round, they are rarely caught in any great quantity in the West Country, where it is more usual to see one or two cod among a catch dominated by pollack, coalfish and ling.

Our most consistent catches of cod come to the inshore boat angler fishing the Eddystone Reef in early spring after the greater launce arrive. These are monster sandeels, often over a foot (30 cm) long and over an inch (2·5 cm) in diameter. Bass, cod and pollack gorge themselves silly on them. There are often a few cod caught each season just below or above 40 lb (18 kg) – short, fat, butter-yellow fish in prime condition as a result of their rich diet of sandeel.

Tackle

For conventional downtide ledgering, 20–30 lb (10–15 kg) class gear is recommended,

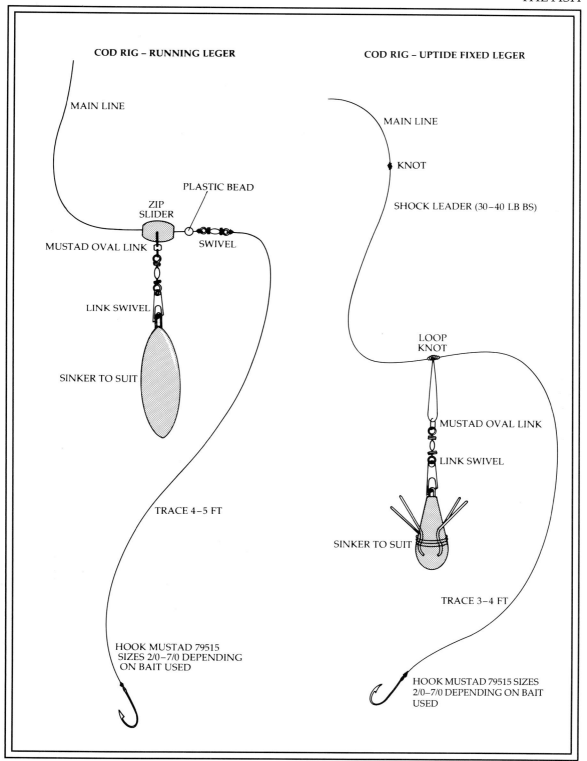

COD RIG – RUNNING LEGER

MAIN LINE

PLASTIC BEAD

ZIP
SLIDER

MUSTAD OVAL LINK

SWIVEL

LINK SWIVEL

SINKER TO SUIT

TRACE 4–5 FT

HOOK MUSTAD 79515
SIZES 2/0–7/0 DEPENDING
ON BAIT USED

COD RIG – UPTIDE FIXED LEGER

MAIN LINE

KNOT

SHOCK LEADER (30–40 LB BS)

LOOP
KNOT

MUSTAD OVAL LINK

LINK SWIVEL

SINKER TO SUIT

TRACE 3–4 FT

HOOK MUSTAD 79515 SIZES
2/0–7/0 DEPENDING ON BAIT
USED

although tackle lighter than this is often used, especially with sandeel bait. Uptide fishing is usually carried out with rods capable of casting 5–6 oz (140–170 gm).

Methods

When a shoal of cod is found in residence over a wreck, many anglers use what has become known as 'killer gear'. This normally consists of a heavy pirk tied direct to the end of the main line, with two or three plastic-skirted Muppets paternostered off the main line. These are sometimes given the added attraction of a strip of mackerel or squid.

More often than not, the rig for downtide fishing will consist of a general-purpose medium-weight running ledger, baited with a mackerel 'flapper' (the backbone is removed by slicing up from the tail) or a whole small squid or two when fishing a deep-water wreck. For fishing broken ground or a shallow-water wreck, the same medium ledger is used, but the bait will invariably be lugworm.

Uptide casting for cod is widely recognized as the supreme method for catching them in the shallower, faster-running waters of estuaries such as the Thames.

A running ledger or fixed-weight ledger is used in conjunction with a breakaway sinker, the fixed-ledger having the edge in deeper, faster-running tides.

Baits

Except in specialized areas such as my own patch in the South West, lugworm is the best cod bait. But cod are catholic eaters and peeler crab, king ragworm, squid, mackerel and herring can all be used.

Hooks

Fine-wire Aberdeens are excellent if you are using light tackle, but generally the Mustad 79515, Real Tackle uptide hooks and the Kamasan hooks are the best hooks for cod. Use sizes 2/0–7/0, depending on the bait.

CONGER EEL

To catch a big conger eel is an ambition shared by most boat anglers. It is a species which combines cunning with sheer brute strength. A big eel will make several powerful dives, so the tackle has to be good and the reel's clutch set up to match the line strength.

On feeling the bite, do not strike, but wait until the eel takes a yard of line, then reel in rapidly to take up the slack, and strike as you feel the weight of the eel. Do not stop – reel in and pump hard until you have it clear of the bottom, as most big eels are lost in these first few seconds of the encounter. Once you have the eel clear of the bottom give no quarter, but if it gets its head down and starts a run, make it fight for every foot of line, but let it run or it will smash your line.

A conger eel which is still very lively, or 'green', can be very dangerous. Make sure an eel is tired out before you bring it aboard. Then put it straight into a fish box or cover the head with a thick, wet sack. This calms it down, until you are ready to deal with it. Be careful, and treat conger which appear to be dead with great caution.

Tackle

A 50 lb (24 kg) class outfit is heavy enough to land the biggest of eels, although with experience and over a wreck which is not too snaggy a 30 lb (15 kg) class outfit is adequate. Choose a rod with a roller tip eye – the stubby 'stand-up' rods are ideal for congering. A lever-drag reel is recommended – the Shimano TLD 25 or 20 fits the bill, the Shimano Beastmaster 12/30 has rapidly become a cult reel with conger fanatics – and the new Penn carbon lever-drag reels are also excellent.

A butt pad is almost essential unless you have the arms of a gorilla. A simple kidney harness can be a great help on a busy day.

Method

A heavy to medium ledger is the best method: a simple running ledger using a zip slider or white nylon sea boom and with a sinker heavy enough to hold bottom. The trace can be flexible wire or 250 lb (115 kg) breaking strain commercial monofilament.

Baits

Probably the best of all conger baits is a mackerel, cut into a 'flapper' (the backbone is removed by slicing up from the tail). Fish such as pout will also serve, and a small bream is a first-class bait.

Squid is an excellent conger bait one day but they won't look at it the next. Even so, it is always worth having some aboard.

Hooks

The best conger hooks I have ever used are the Mustad Sea Demons, followed by the Sea Master, which are much more expensive. The standard O'Shaughnessey are also good hooks, as are the chromed Partridge Z22s. Sizes vary between 8/0 and 12/0 depending on the size of the bait. I prefer big baits, so I use size 10/0 or 12/0.

FLOUNDER

The flounder is one of the smallest species which pursued with any degree of dedication by the small boat angler. It can provide an interesting day's fishing during those cold, bright days that we occasionally get during the winter.

Tackle

You can use the lightest of tackle for flounder because you would have to be very lucky to catch one at 3 lb (1·5 kg). Your spinning rod and fixed-spool reel with 8 lb (3·5 kg) line is more than adequate. Using this tackle you can fish uptide or downtide, or even floatfish if the opportunity presents itself.

Methods

From November until the heavy frosts drive the crabs out into deeper water, using a light running ledger can be problematical because the crabs will attack your bait as soon as it is near the bottom. The answer is to incorporate a small polystyrene float into the trace to keep the bait just off the bottom and clear of the crabs.

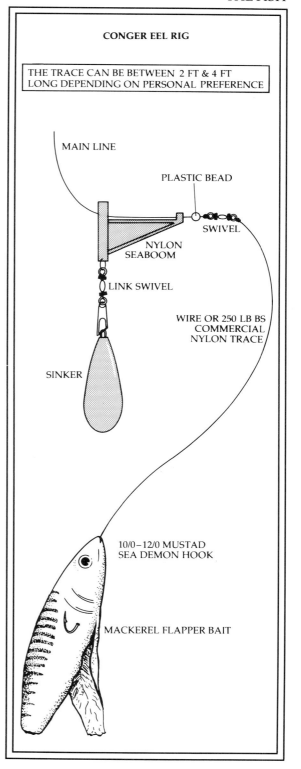

CONGER EEL RIG

THE TRACE CAN BE BETWEEN 2 FT & 4 FT LONG DEPENDING ON PERSONAL PREFERENCE

MAIN LINE

PLASTIC BEAD

SWIVEL

NYLON SEABOOM

LINK SWIVEL

WIRE OR 250 LB BS COMMERCIAL NYLON TRACE

SINKER

10/0–12/0 MUSTAD SEA DEMON HOOK

MACKEREL FLAPPER BAIT

FLOUNDER FLOAT RIG

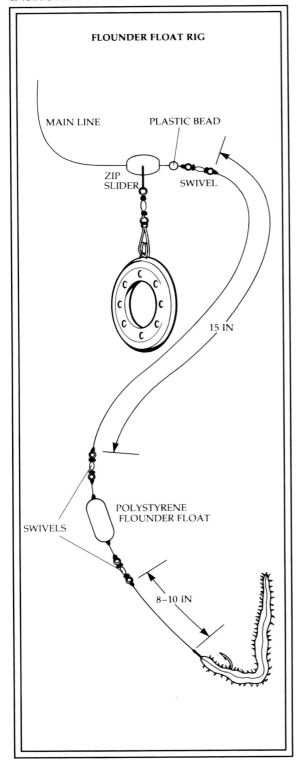

MAIN LINE

PLASTIC BEAD

ZIP SLIDER

SWIVEL

15 IN

POLYSTYRENE FLOUNDER FLOAT

SWIVELS

8–10 iN

A zip slider is used to clip the sinker to the main line. The trace is about 3 ft (0·9 m). Eighteen inches (45 cm) from the hook tie a swivel, then a short length of line 5–6 in (13–15 cm) long. Slide the flounder float onto this length of line, then a small bead and another swivel, and from this swivel tie in the hook length of about 10 in (25 cm). Fished downtide this is a very efficient rig, and the bite is signalled very clearly to the rod tip.

After the frosts are upon us and the crabs are gone, the flounder float is no longer necessary, and the normal light running ledger will work well. This method is ideal for fishing on the drift, provided the speed of the drift is not too great. If it is, then going to anchor and using a heavier sinker will be necessary to hold the bait down.

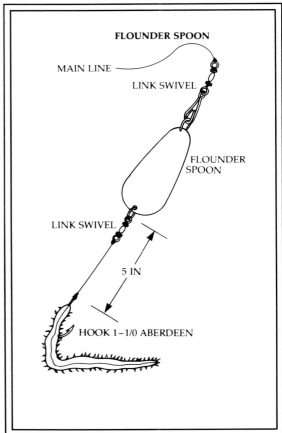

FLOUNDER SPOON

MAIN LINE

LINK SWIVEL

FLOUNDER SPOON

LINK SWIVEL

5 IN

HOOK 1–1/0 ABERDEEN

It is easy enough to flip this rig uptide and fish it as you would an uptide rig with a lightly loaded rod tip and wait for a slack-line bite.

An alternative technique which works well in shallow water is the use of a flounder spoon. This is a specially made metal spoon-like lure, with swivels clipped to both extremities. The swivel at the pointed end of the spoon is tied to the main line. About 5–6 in (13–15 cm) of line is tied to the swivel at the other end and then to your hook.

The spoon hook is baited with harbour rag and the spoon dropped over the downtide side of the boat. Wait until the spoon has tapped the bottom, let it fish for a minute or two, slowly lift and lower the rod a couple of times, let it fish for a couple of minutes, lift the rod and let the spoon flutter downtide a few more yards until it finds the bottom again. By repeating this process you will sometimes have 70–80 yards (64–73 m) of line out. Surprisingly, even at extreme range the flounder's rat-tat-tat bite can be distinctly felt. Spooning is a very old flounder-fishing method which is about due to be rediscovered.

A final tip: some anglers swear by attractors in the form of brightly coloured beads threaded onto the line just above the hook. I often use them myself when floundering.

Baits
Peeler crab and ordinary small harbour ragworm have always been my best flounder baits.

Hooks
Size 1 and 1/0 Aberdeens are excellent flounder hooks, but take care not to overload the hook with bait, otherwise the hook point will be masked when the fish picks it up.

LING
Big Ling are found on or near deepwater wrecks. They are a predatory fish with sharp teeth and can grow to over 50 lb (24 kg) in weight. On the wrecks, the average weight will be between 20–30 lb (9–14 kg), and often if the ling are in residence it will be possible to fill the boat with them.

Ling are not the most difficult of fish to catch and little skill or finesse is required. The tackle needs to be strong and serviceable. A 30 lb (14 kg) class outfit is heavy enough to subdue the largest of ling, because they are not hard fighters, but they do use the currents to put pressure on your tackle. When playing a deep water ling, keep a steady pressure on against the curve of the rod and recover line by pumping the rod, reeling in on the downward movement of the rod.

Disgorge the hook by jumping it out. Never be tempted to put your hand too close to the ling's teeth. Check your trace line for abrasion, nicks etc and if damage is evident, put on new end tackle: you could find that a big conger is your next adversary.

Reef or open ground ling are generally smaller than those found on the wrecks. The reef ling are reputed to taste better than some of the big old wreck fish.

Tackle
A 30 lb (13·5 kg) class general purpose outfit will serve well. On a day when a good catch is being made, one of the new stand-up rods and a Shimano 2 speed Beastmaster reel will prove their worth.

Method
Use a heavy duty running ledger with either a zip slider or nylon boom. Use a 3 ft (0·9 m) trace of, say, 40 lb (18 kg) monofilament, with a short length of 250 lb (110 kg) monofilament or wire to the hook. This short length can be made detachable by means of a heavy duty link swivel. If the hook has been swallowed by the fish, it is then the work of a moment to unclip this short length and replace it with another short end trace.

Best baits
Ling are a scavenging fish and virtually any bait will catch them, but perhaps the most success-

ful bait is either a side of mackerel or a mackerel flapper (ie a mackerel with its backbone removed).

Best hooks

The Mustad Sea Demon is probably the best hook for its hooking power, but being short in the shank can be difficult to remove. The O'Shaughnessey is a favourite, about size 8/0 to 10/0.

MACKEREL

There are two reasons for catching mackerel. The first is for bait, when we use a set of mackerel feathers and catch them six or seven at a time. This is fun and the mackerel makes a wonderful bait for other species of fish, but do your bit for conservation by not taking more than you need. The second reason is that ounce for ounce mackerel are one of the hardest-fighting fish in the sea and on ultra-light tackle are a worthy adversary.

Tackle

When using a standard set of seven feathers a 20 or 30 lb (10 or 15 kg) class outfit is ideal. Use a pound (0·45 kg) of lead and work the feathers by a pumping action, jigging them up and down a few feet at a time. Use the 'countdown' technique: drop the feathers over the side and watch them till they just disappear from sight, work the rod up and down a few times, there are often mackerel in the shade of the boat. Then release the spool and allow the feathers to drop, counting to five, work the feathers, wait another five seconds, drop, work the feathers, and so on until you reach the bottom. Coming up, give seven turns on the reel handle, work the feathers and so on. This way the water's depth is systematically searched for the shoaling mackerel.

Shop-bought feathers often have far too much feather on them. Use a pair of scissors to ruthlessly trim them back to about a ¼ in (6 mm) longer than the hook. Also trim the body so that each feather could be described as

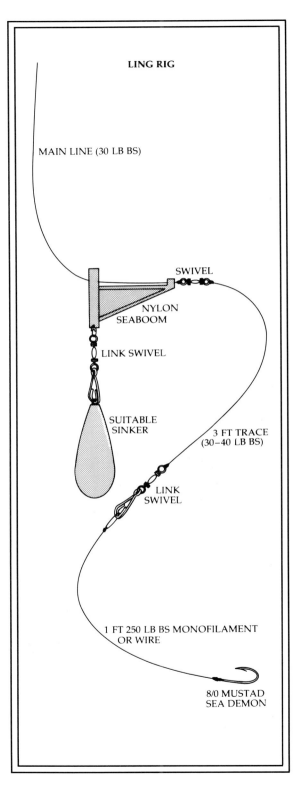

LING RIG

MAIN LINE (30 LB BS)

SWIVEL

NYLON
SEABOOM

LINK SWIVEL

SUITABLE
SINKER

3 FT TRACE
(30–40 LB BS)

LINK
SWIVEL

1 FT 250 LB BS MONOFILAMENT
OR WIRE

8/0 MUSTAD
SEA DEMON

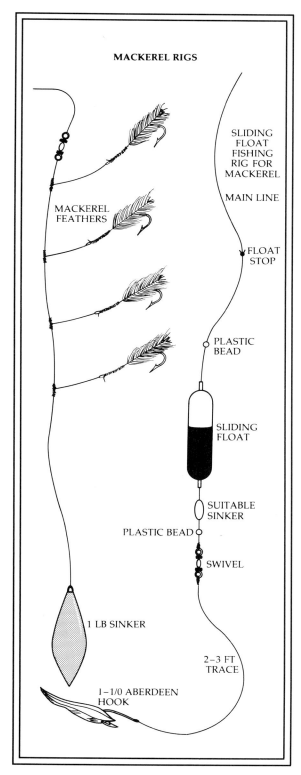

MACKEREL RIGS

SLIDING FLOAT FISHING RIG FOR MACKEREL

MAIN LINE

MACKEREL FEATHERS

FLOAT STOP

PLASTIC BEAD

SLIDING FLOAT

SUITABLE SINKER

PLASTIC BEAD

SWIVEL

1 LB SINKER

2–3 FT TRACE

1–1/0 ABERDEEN HOOK

sparse. Use at least a pound (0·45 kg) of weight, since if you can see the shoal on the echo-sounder you need to get right down to them. A light sinker will be swept away in the current and the fish will probably not see your feathers.

Catching mackerel one at a time on an ultra-light spinning rod and 6–7 lb (2·7–3 kg) line is fine fun. I enjoy a bit of sport with mackerel when there is a flat calm and every other species of fish seems to have gone looking for a shady spot.

Mackerel can be caught by spinning with a small shiny metal lure such as ABU Toby and Krill. Small plugs will also provide some good sport. But floatfishing with a thin strip of silver mackerel skin or a side from a sandeel hooked once through the apex is a relaxing and worth-while way of spending an afternoon afloat. You will occasionally catch a garfish when using a float like this, and a strip from this fish is an excellent bait for mackerel and pollack.

Tackle
For feathering use a 20–30 lb (10–15 kg) conventional boat rod and reel. For floatfishing and spinning use a two-handed 8–10 ft (2·5–3 m) spinning rod with a small to medium-sized fixed-spool reel.

Baits
Thin strips of silver mackerel or garfish, or san-deel hooked once through the apex.

Lures
ABU Toby or Krill. Mackerel feathers.

MULLET

Mullet are a species which many boat anglers tend to forget, but by using your boat you can often visit places which the shore angler simply cannot get to, such as offshore breakwaters and inaccessible coves and islands. Mullet fishing is not nearly as difficult as many would have you believe, but to score a success usually requires planning.

If you know a place frequented by mullet

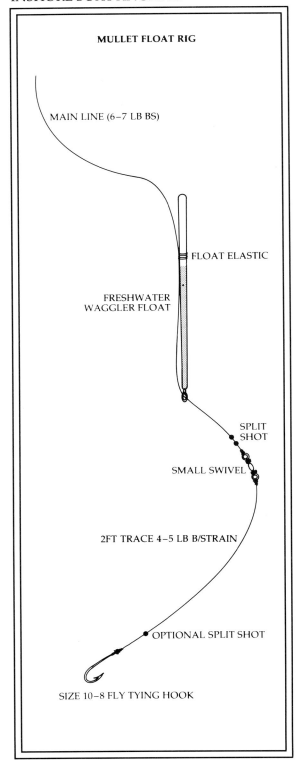

MULLET FLOAT RIG

MAIN LINE (6–7 LB BS)

FLOAT ELASTIC

FRESHWATER
WAGGLER FLOAT

SPLIT
SHOT

SMALL SWIVEL

2FT TRACE 4–5 LB B/STRAIN

OPTIONAL SPLIT SHOT

SIZE 10–8 FLY TYING HOOK

shoals, then groundbaiting in advance will pay real dividends. My most successful groundbait consists of minced mackerel, mixed with bread and stirred together in a bucket. Put a bucketful into a fine-meshed net and suspend it under a small buoy, held in position with something like a sash-cord weight or a lump of scrap metal. Groundbait on Saturday, fish on Sunday, is my routine and it is surprising how well it works. Put a float out with a prawn as well, the groundbait will attract the mullet, which in turn attract the bass. Bass often swim with a mullet shoal anyway.

Method
Ultra-light float gear using a freshwater angler's 'Waggler' float, the larger sizes of which can carry a surprising amount of lead and can be cast quite well. Free lining can be deadly.

Tackle
Many anglers use freshwater carp rods for mullet fishing. I use my 10 ft (3 m) Tekno Bass Spinning rod which is excellent for this purpose. A small fixed spool loaded with 6–7 lb (2·7–3 kg) monofilament completes the outfit. I like to use the smallest Shimano Baitrunner fixed spool, because of its unique ability to allow a fish to run off with a bait, then with a half-turn of the handle, set the hook.

Best baits
The best bait will depend on where you fish, but bread and/or mashed mackerel has always produced good fishing for me. It is important that previous groundbaiting has been carried out in order that you have established a feeding pattern.

You can go on the day, groundbait and catch fish, but my best days and biggest fish have come when I have carried out previous groundbaiting. Nip a breadflake over the eye of your hook, dunk it in the water for a second or two, lift it out and gently squeeze the breadflake to remove the air trapped in the bread. Drop over the side of the boat and allow it to trot back to where the groundbait is being dispersed; the fish will take the breadflake quite hard, pulling the waggler float way under.

If you choose to use mackerel flesh, don't cut a piece and hang it on the hook, find a fresh piece and with the hook just tear at the flesh until you have a little ball of bait just big enough to conceal the hook, make sure the hook point is not masked.

Hooks

Hooks need to be small by sea angling standards, but at the same time strong. I have found the best hooks to be those used by trout fishermen to tie their flies on. Size 10s and 8s are just right, there are numerous patterns available but the basic 'Model Perfect' fly hook is very good. Mini–Trebles size 12s are sometimes used, especially if using mackerel flesh baits. I have used these hooks myself in the past, but lately I have had reservations about using them, preferring to use the single hook.

The average size of the mullet caught from a boat is often larger than the shore average. Make sure you have a good landing net and don't keep fish you do not need.

PLAICE

Plaice are one of the inshore boat angler's favourite species. They move inshore in April/ May, the first of the season's inshore migrations and are especially welcome as an indication that the new season has at last begun.

Fishing with light tackle, the plaice can give a good account of itself, as it artfully uses the span of its body as a kite in the current to exert every bit of pressure against your line. The sight of an early Spring Plaice gliding up through the clean green water toward the waiting net, is indeed one to gladden the heart of any angler.

Tackle

The tackle for conventional downtide fishing can be as light as the 8 lb (3·5 kg) class, but most anglers choose to use a 12 lb outfit, mainly be-

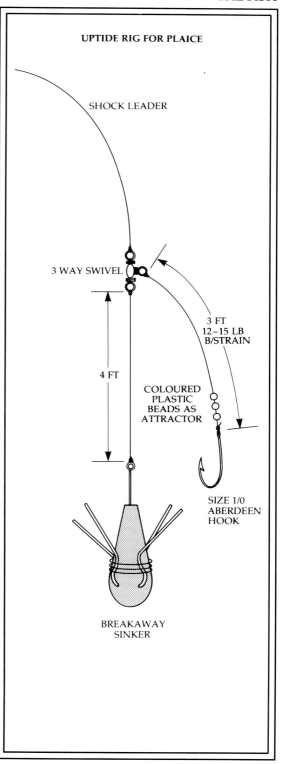

UPTIDE RIG FOR PLAICE

SHOCK LEADER

3 WAY SWIVEL

3 FT
12–15 LB
B/STRAIN

4 FT

COLOURED
PLASTIC
BEADS AS
ATTRACTOR

SIZE 1/0
ABERDEEN
HOOK

BREAKAWAY
SINKER

cause it can cope better with the strain of re-trieving sinkers which might weigh up to 12 ounces (340 g), plus maybe a fish, in the heavy tides which plaice seem to like. Reels for this style of fishing can be the Shimano TLD 5, Penn 2/0, ABU 9000, 7000, etc.

Method

The bottom rig is not at all complicated, simply a Zip slider onto the main line, stopped by bead and swivel. From the swivel, use an 8–10 ft (2·5–3 m) trace to the hook. I like to put another swivel in the trace, 2–3 ft up from the hook.

The classic sinker for plaice fishing is the old-fashioned but highly effective 'Watch lead', so called because of its superficial resemblance to an old-fashioned pocket watch. The Watch lead seems to be particularly suited to the shell and sand bottom favoured by plaice. Use just enough weight to hold bottom, fish for a few minutes, tighten up just enough to lift the sink-er off the bottom, pause for a second or two to feel for a sneaky bite, and allow the current to take your sinker downtide a few more yards, fish for a few minutes, and so on. This is known as 'walking' your sinker.

Uptide fishing for plaice

I tend to favour a light 3–5 oz (85–141 gm) up-tide casting outfit with 3, 4, or 5 oz (85–115 or 140 gm) Breakaway sinkers, depending on the strength of the tide. You do not have to use so much weight as you would with more conven-tional sinkers, because the Breakaway wires sink into the softish bottom and grip. I use a three-way swivel 3 ft (0·9 m) from the sinker and a 3 ft (0·9 m) trace from the swivel.

After casting and with the sinker settled into position, gently wind in just enough line to put a curve into the tip of the rod, then put the rod in a rod holder. The bite will be a 'slack line' bite, which indicates that the fish has hooked itself and tripped the breakaway sinker at the same time.

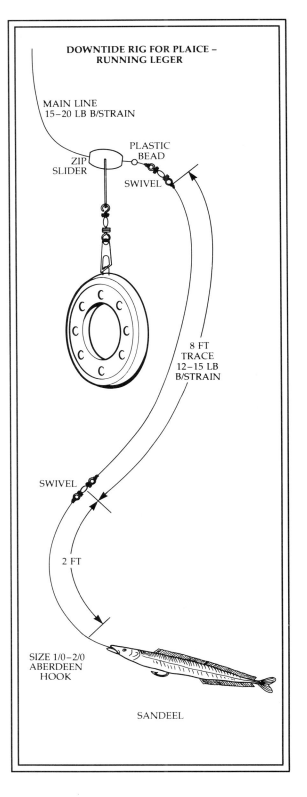

DOWNTIDE RIG FOR PLAICE – RUNNING LEGER

MAIN LINE 15–20 LB B/STRAIN

ZIP SLIDER

PLASTIC BEAD

SWIVEL

8 FT TRACE 12–15 LB B/STRAIN

SWIVEL

2 FT

SIZE 1/0–2/0 ABERDEEN HOOK

SANDEEL

Lloyd Saunders of Dartmouth holds aloft two fine plaice caught from his own boat Saltwind. *Bait was a cocktail of peeler crab and squid strip fished hard on the bottom of the Skerries Bank, near Start Point in south Devon.*

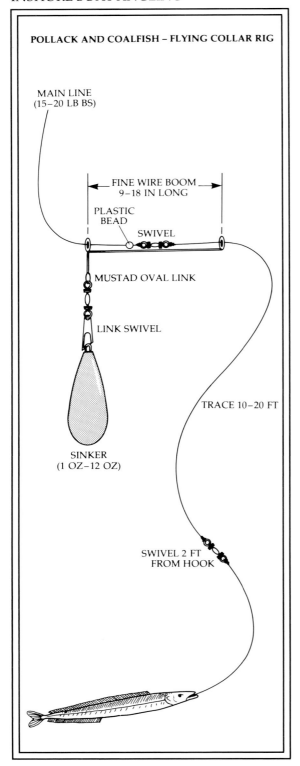

POLLACK AND COALFISH – FLYING COLLAR RIG

MAIN LINE
(15–20 LB BS)

FINE WIRE BOOM
9–18 IN LONG

PLASTIC
BEAD

SWIVEL

MUSTAD OVAL LINK

LINK SWIVEL

TRACE 10–20 FT

SINKER
(1 OZ–12 OZ)

SWIVEL 2 FT
FROM HOOK

Baits

Early season, that is before the sandeels arrive, the bait which seems to be the best is a cocktail of peeler crab and squid, lugworm and squid or king ragworm and squid. Peeler crab and squid is in my view the best. Take half a peeled peeler crab, thread it onto the hook and bind into place with elasticated cotton. Cut your squid into strips about 6–7 in (15–18 cm) long by a ¼ in (0·5 cm) wide. Nick a piece of squid onto the hook by passing the point of the hook through one end, once only, so that the squid hangs nicely in the bend of the hook, with the crab above it.

I don't know what the plaice take this crab/squid cocktail to be, (I suspect razorfish), but I can vouch for the fact that it works. As the season goes on, sandeels become the plaice's major diet, and often nothing else will do.

Hooks

Aberdeens size 1/0 or 2/0; that's it, there is nothing better.

POLLACK AND COALFISH

To all intents and purposes, the angler can consider these two species of fish as being identical. Both are fine sporting fish, with probably the coalfish having the edge in terms of speed and stamina. They can both be caught over wreck and reefs, both offshore and inshore.

Wreck

The pollack are often seen during the winter months clouding the screen of your Echo sounder just uptide of the wreck. The best method is to start your drift well uptide of the wreck, allowing sufficient time for your lures to be working at the correct depth, before the fish start to show on your sounder. Pollack and coalfish can be heaved over the side on killer gear, ie a heavy pirk, and two – I've even seen six – Eddystone Eels. This brute force fishing is in my view unnecessary and unsporting, and I will not fish aboard a boat that advocates this method. A 20 lb (9 kg) class outfit with a

A nice little reef-caught Pollack, held by my friend Vic Mozolics. Sandeel bait fished on a long flowing trace over the rocky pinnacles is a deadly method for these fish.

medium ledger using a fine wire boom and a long 12 ft (3·5 m) trace is an ideal sporting set of tackle. Lighter tackle makes the most of these sporting species.

Reef

Reef fishing for pollack is to me, one of the immeasurable joys of running your own boat. A good day out on a reef, with light tackle and some co-operative pollack, sorts out my psyche!

A carbon spinning rod between 7–9 ft (2–2·7 m) can be matched with a mini multiplier and 10 lb (4·5 kg) BS line, to give the fish a chance to show what it can do. The end rig can be a fine wire boom carrying between 1 and 6 ounces of lead, depending on where you are fishing and the strength of the tide. The trace length can vary from 10 ft (3 m) on big tides up to 20 ft (6 m) on weak neap tides.

Inshore

Pollack are excellent shallow water fish and a 10 lb (4·5 kg) pollack caught in 10 ft (3 m) of water can be a real demon of a fighter, especially if you have tempted it by freelining or floatfishing a live sandeel or prawn. Spinning with plugs, leadheads or metal lures will also tempt these fish, and do they get mad when they realize they have been fooled!

Be careful in your boat when you get in close after these fish, check your chart for rocks which will be near the surface and if you have any doubts, anchor off and cast in.

Tackle

For wreck fishing, a 20 lb (9 kg) class outfit, light lever drag reel such as the Shimano TLD 10.

For reef fishing, 16 or 12 lb class rods are excellent. Light lever drag reel Shimano TLD 5 or else the ABU 8500 or 7000.

For inshore fishing, use 7–10 ft (2–3 m) carbon fibre spinning rods. ABU, Daiwa and Shakespeare make some excellent rods. Do not make the mistake of buying a floppy rod, it needs to be able to handle 10 lb (4·5 kg) line and

to make it work. Small multipliers such as the Shimano Bantams, ABU XLT's and Daiwa Millionairs are all reels capable of landing good fish. Fixed spool reels for this type of fishing have to be a bit tougher than average, yet have a fast retrieve and a sensitive clutch. Some of the new lever drag systems on fixed spool reels are excellent for inshore fishing.

Best baits

King ragworm is a superb bait, especially early season over the reefs and inshore. Live sandeel are excellent bait over reefs and inshore, but they don't last too long in deep water. Joey Mackerel, (baby mackerel caught in the Winter months) are a deadly bait for big pollack and coalfish. (Late bass go crazy for them as well.) Mackerel strip, properly cut and presented, is a brilliant bait over wreck, reef *and* inshore.

Prawns, caught with a drop net over the side of the quay, are greatly underestimated as an inshore bait.

Hooks

Generally fine wire Aberdeens between 2/0 and 7/0, depending on bait. Mustad 6/0 and 7/0 Aberdeens are made from a heavier wire and are thus particularly suited to bait fishing over wrecks.

Lures

Virtually every lure ever made will at some time or other find a pollack willing to have a go at it. Plastic eels and plugs are the most successful lures inshore. Eddystone Eels and Redgill plastic eels are the supreme lures over the deep water wrecks and reefs, particularly red and black coloured eels.

RAY

Thornback, blonde, and small-eyed ray are the main species of ray sought by anglers, of which the small-eyed ray is the smallest and liveliest. Many a bass angler has found a small-eyed ray on his hook instead of the bass the determined runs had led him to expect. Ray are often quite

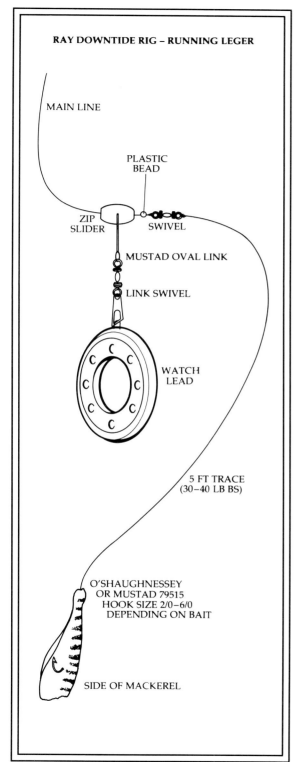

RAY DOWNTIDE RIG – RUNNING LEGER

MAIN LINE

PLASTIC
BEAD

ZIP
SLIDER

SWIVEL

MUSTAD OVAL LINK

LINK SWIVEL

WATCH
LEAD

5 FT TRACE
(30–40 LB BS)

O'SHAUGHNESSEY
OR MUSTAD 79515
HOOK SIZE 2/0–6/0
DEPENDING ON BAIT

SIDE OF MACKEREL

localized and they will frequently return year after year to the same sandbank. So if you catch one ray, it is well worth investigating the adjacent area thoroughly, and taking a careful note of your position.

Ray fishing is often a waiting game, more so than for many other species. I tend to give them a couple of hours and if I haven't caught one, try for something else.

Tackle

This depends on the depth of water which you are fishing. My simple rule of thumb is shallow water, say up to 50 ft (15 m) – fish uptide. Over 50 ft (15 m) fish conventional downtide; this is not a cast-iron rule, but it seems to be effective in my experience.

For uptide fishing, use a rod capable of casting 4–6 oz (110–170 gm), matched with Shimano TSM 2 FSC, ABU 7000, etc, loaded with 15–18 lb (6·5–8 kg) breaking strain line, plus shock leader. Or use conventional Downtide, 20 lb (9 kg) class rod matched with Shimano TLD 20, ABU 9000, Penn Longbeach 65 or Mitchell 624.

Method

Uptide running ledger using zip slider with the Breakaway sinker on 5 ft (1·5 m) of line from the slider; use the same breaking strain line as your shock leader.

Your trace needs to be of a reasonable breaking strain, 30–40 lbs (13·5–18 kg), to withstand the abrasion of the ray's crushing jaws and the inevitable contact with sand and shingle which goes with ray fishing. The trace should be about 4 ft (1·2 m) long.

Downtide conventional fishing is nearly always carried out at anchor after finding the spot with Echo Sounder and Decca or Transits.

End tackle is a medium-weight running ledger using a zip Slider with a sinker such as that old faithful, the Watch lead; but make sure it is heavy enough to hold bottom. Stop the slider with bead and swivel and about a 5 ft (1·5 m) trace of 30–40 lb (13·5–18 kg) monofilament

Uptide casting with peeler crab bait accounted for this thornback ray. Ray Dower and I were fishing a mark just inside the breakwater at Plymouth.

works well. Do not be in too much of a hurry to strike, the ray will settle over the bait and take its time having a good old munch. You will see your rod tip bouncing and twitching and the urge will be to pick up your rod and strike. But wait until the ray starts to move off, then pick up the rod and point it down the line, reeling until you feel the weight of the fish, and then lift the rod to set the hook.

Best baits

For thornback ray, sandeel, mackerel fillet, peeler crab, occasionally king ragworm or squid. Small-eyed ray will take live sandeel, frozen sandeel, mackerel strip or razorfish. Blonde ray can be caught with live sandeel, frozen sandeel, razorfish, squid, lugworm, mackerel strip, or cocktail combinations of these.

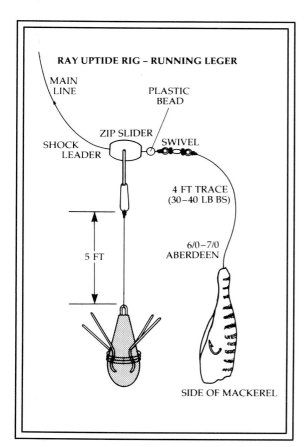

RAY UPTIDE RIG – RUNNING LEGER

MAIN LINE

PLASTIC BEAD

ZIP SLIDER

SHOCK LEADER

SWIVEL

4 FT TRACE (30–40 LB BS)

6/0–7/0 ABERDEEN

5 FT

SIDE OF MACKEREL

Hooks

Thornback and blonde ray need a reasonably strong hook, favourites are O'Shaughnessey and Mustad 79515 patterns, size 2/0 – 6/0, depending on bait used. Small-eyed ray are often caught using a slightly lighter hook, especially when using sandeel baits. Aberdeens, Real Tackle uptide hooks, and Spearpoint Boat hooks are excellent Small-eyed ray hooks. Whatever pattern you choose to use, keep your hooks sharp: ray are difficult enough to hook at the best of times, without handicapping yourself.

Use your echo sounder and charts to choose the right sort of bottom. Thornback ray prefer a muddy bottom while Small-eyed ray will be found on sandy bottom, usually near rocky outcrops. Blonde ray have a liking for sand and shell sandbanks swept by a heavy tidal run. Rays will often kite up to the surface well astern of the boat. Most fish are lost bringing them to the boat near the surface, so be particularly careful at that stage. Gaff ray in the wing and they can be returned virtually unharmed.

GENERAL ADVICE FOR SHARK

Catching sharks from your own boat, without the comforting thought that there will be a charter boat skipper to gaff the shark and get it inboard, is not a proposition to be undertaken lightly.

Evidently, if you have just a 14 ft (4 m) Sea Hog or such a craft, bringing a 7 ft (2 m) shark aboard could have some interesting ramifications. But as we all know, most anglers have that extra dimension in their makeup which makes them want to get close to the wild and even the dangerous. In recent years, sharking success for me has meant fighting the shark to the side of the boat, touching the shark with my hand, and shaking the hook out, releasing the fish. I know many others who do the same. If however the fish is a big one, maybe a record or competition winner, then I believe it to be fair game.

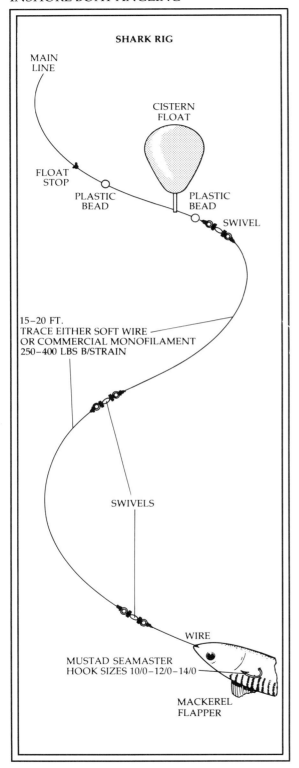

SHARK RIG

MAIN
LINE

CISTERN
FLOAT

FLOAT
STOP

PLASTIC
BEAD

PLASTIC
BEAD

SWIVEL

15–20 FT.
TRACE EITHER SOFT WIRE
OR COMMERCIAL MONOFILAMENT
250–400 LBS B/STRAIN

SWIVELS

WIRE

MUSTAD SEAMASTER
HOOK SIZES 10/0–12/0–14/0

MACKEREL
FLAPPER

Blue and porbeagle sharks are the inshore boat angler's big game fishing. Indeed, the biggest fish I have ever seen landed was hooked 100 yards (90 m) off a beach full of swimmers!

Method
The basic method is float fishing; the float can consist of a partly inflated balloon or a plastic ball of the type used in flush valves. My favourite floats are the plastic ones used along the top of gill nets.

The line slides through the float or through a swivel tied to the float until the set depth is reached, this depth can be anything between 10–100 ft (3–30 m). If there are two or three of you fishing, each of you should fish at a different depth until the shark are found.

The trace is usually soft wire or heavy duty monofilament exceeding 300 lbs (135 kg) breaking strain and a minimum of 15 ft (4·5 m) in length. This is to withstand the shark's teeth and the very abrasive effects of the shark's skin. Two – preferably three – swivels should be incorporated into the trace, in case the shark performs its favourite twist and roll tricks as it gets close to the boat.

If you know you are not going to keep the shark, avoid gaffing or lifting the fish out of the water. If you can see the hook in the fish's jaw then you can easily jump the hook out by using a long-handled hook jumper. Grab the first swivel in the trace, put the jumper hook around the trace wire and slide the jumper down to the bend of the hook, lift with the jumper and pull down with the line held in the other hand. The fish's weight and movement will usually shake the hook loose. On the other hand, if the hook is evidently well down inside the shark, don't even try to get the hook out. Cut the trace as close as possible and leave the shark to get rid of the hook naturally: they are surprisingly good at it!

Tackle
A 50 lb (23 kg) class outfit will easily handle the largest sharks that swim in British waters, in-

Brian Taylor's world record porbeagle shark weighed in at 382 lbs and was caught on 8-k. (17.6 lbs) breaking strain line. It was not an easy task getting it inboard.

Brian Taylor played his world record porbeagle for over three hours before the fish could be brought aboard. This fish was first hooked less than 400 yd from the shore, off the north coast of Cornwall.

cluding porbeagle and mako. A 30 lb (13·5 kg) class outfit would be more sporting, even if there was a chance of a porbeagle or a long-shot chance of a mako.

Most of the shark fishing done around our shores is for blue shark and in all honesty a 20 lb (9 kg) class outfit could easily handle the largest of blue sharks found in British waters. Start with a 30 lb (13·5 kg) outfit, catch a few shark and graduate to a 20 lb (9 kg) class rod and reel so that you can enjoy shark fishing for the sport of it.

Tackle

Good 20 and 30 lb class rods are made by all the major manufacturers, but a roller tip eye on the rod is good to have. If you can afford it, get yourself a lever drag reel like the Shimano TLD 25 or 20, which will double for all your heavy fishing, (Conger etc) and will perform superbly well when sharking.

Best baits

Without doubt the best bait is mackerel. There is some difference of opinion as to whether old and smelly mackerel is to be preferred to fresh, I prefer fresh myself. The whole mackerel is hooked so that the barb of the hook protrudes and is not masked in any way.

'Rubby Dubby' is the name given to the minced and mashed fish which is put into a fine meshed net and hung over the side of the boat so that the oil, blood and particles form a 'slick'. Your floated baits are arranged to fish in this slick, from a few yards to 50 yards (45 m) from the boat. It is very bad manners to drive your boat through a slick emanating from a boat which is obviously shark fishing.

Hooks

The classic shark hook is the Mustad Seamaster and most anglers who make up, say, half a dozen shark traces, are willing to pay a few pounds for these hand-finished, forged hooks. They are worth every penny, because even after a shark has ruined the trace, the hook is cut off, dried, sharpened and used to make a new trace. I tend to use large hooks say, 12/0 or 14/0 Seamasters, because usually these large hooks are not swallowed and can be 'jumped' out of the shark's jaw.

Sharks can give a fine day's sport, but you cannot eat them, so avoid killing them. If you have to get a shark into your boat, control the tail, this will control the fish. If in any doubt about your ability to remove the hook, leave it and use another trace.

TOPE

The tope is a member of the shark family and like the blue shark is pursued by anglers almost wholly for its sporting qualities, I have never met anyone who has eaten a tope!

I believe that a tope actually fights harder than a blue shark, size for size. The tope bite is usually indicated by the fish picking up the bait and going off on a short run; after a slight pause off it goes on a long searing run, which is very much part of the excitement of tope fishing. This behaviour is typical of shark tactics. The pick up and short run is to kill the baitfish, the pause is to turn the baitfish to swallow it head first, so that the baitfish fins are folded flat as the shark swallows. The shark then discovers the line restricting its movement and takes off on a prolonged, violent run.

As anglers who intend to return the fish we have a responsibility to prevent the tope from swallowing the hook deeply. So the time to strike is almost immediately after the fish has finished the initial short run. You may well lose the occasional fish by striking at this moment, but you must balance this loss against the needless killing of the fish. Striking at the pause will result in a majority of liphooked fish, which can be released by jumping the hook free, avoiding the distress caused by lifting the fish out of the water.

Tackle

Tope can be caught by conventional boatfishing downtide, as well as the uptide method. An

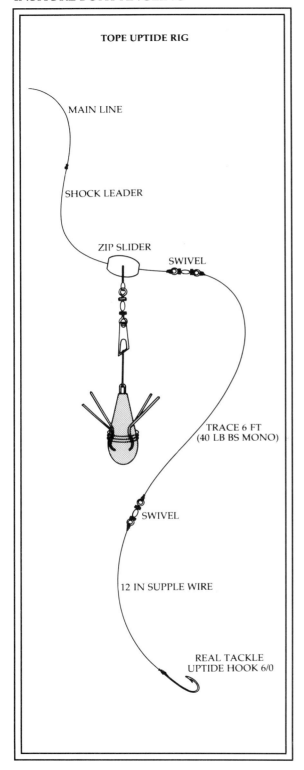

TOPE UPTIDE RIG

MAIN LINE

SHOCK LEADER

ZIP SLIDER

SWIVEL

TRACE 6 FT
(40 LB BS MONO)

SWIVEL

12 IN SUPPLE WIRE

REAL TACKLE
UPTIDE HOOK 6/0

Uptide outfit capable of casting 5–8 oz (140–225 gm) sinkers is ideal and while fully capable of landing large tope, will still give lesser fish a chance to show their paces. The Shimano TSM 2 FSC and ABU 7000 reels loaded with 15–18 lb (6·5–8 kg) breaking strain line are universally employed by devotees of tope fishing.

Method
Conventional Downtide end tackle is simply a zip slider or nylon seaboom to carry the sinker, with the main line threaded through and stopped by bead and swivel. The trace can be 10–12 ft (3–3·5 m) long, consisting of 7 or 8 ft (2–2·5 m) of 100 lb (45 kg) commercial nylon, to a swivel, and from this swivel, 3 or 4 ft (0·9–1·2 m) of 100 lb (45 kg) soft wire to the hook. I tend to use these heavier breaking strains because they are easier to grab and hold when jumping the hook.

The Uptide rig is simple enough, but you will have to use a heavy duty shock leader for casting, and to withstand the abrasive effects of the tope's skin, should the fish roll on the line. Use a 15–20 ft (4·5–6 m) shock leader of 40–50 lb (18–23 kg) breaking strain monofilament, tied to the main line with an improved blood or uni knot. A zip slider fits onto the shock leader, and a swivel is tied to the other end. The trace itself is tied to that swivel and consists of 6 ft (1·8 m) of 40 lb (18 kg) monofilament ending with another swivel. From this swivel is a 12 in (30 cm) length of supple 30–35 lb wire to the hook.

Using this uptide rig is simplicity itself, but its effectiveness depends on using a reasonably heavy Breakaway type sinker, with longer than normal grip wires. What happens is that the tope picks up the bait and runs off against a lightly set drag and ratchet. The fish can only run for the length of the shock leader because the knot where the shock leader joins the main line will not pass through the slider hole. At this point the fish drives the hook home by its own momentum and weight, tripping the Breakaway sinker at the same time.

A 74-lb blue shark caught on 12 lb breaking strain line, a British light tackle club record, which still stands.

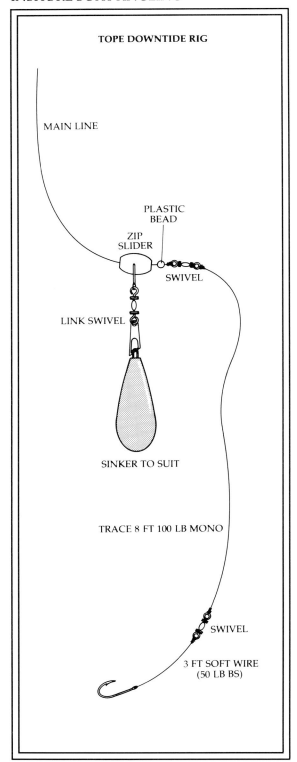

TOPE DOWNTIDE RIG

MAIN LINE

PLASTIC BEAD

ZIP SLIDER

SWIVEL

LINK SWIVEL

SINKER TO SUIT

TRACE 8 FT 100 LB MONO

SWIVEL

3 FT SOFT WIRE (50 LB BS)

Reel rapidly until you feel the weight of the fish, and give a firm strike just to make sure; this method results in a high percentage of lip hooked fish, ensuring a quick and easy release.

Best baits
Bait is not difficult: use whole side of mackerel or a mackerel flapper, whole small pout or whiting, or half a smallish flatfish, dabs for preference. The best bait in estuarial waters is a small freshwater eel or chunks of a larger one; greater sandeel works just as well.

Hooks
Sizes 4/0 to 7/0 medium weight wire hooks. The Mustad 6/0 and 7/0 Aberdeens are made from a heavier gauge wire than the smaller sizes. These are excellent hooks for tope. Also, the Real Tackle uptide hooks made by Partridge are superbly sharp and strong for their size and are eminently suitable for this style of tope fishing.

A playful blue shark tried all day to grab our rubby dubby sacks of minced mackerel. It finally got one and ripped the sack to shreds with one bite.

TURBOT

Turbot are almost a mystical fish to many anglers, difficult to find and not easy to catch. Only a small percentage of anglers have ever caught a turbot and very few indeed have ever caught one over 10 lbs (4·5 kg) in weight. It is this elusive quality, the rarity factor, which will often motivate anglers to spend days fishing hard for this fish, with little reward.

It is not all waiting however; when drifting or anchored over an offshore sand and shell bank, which is the favoured habitat of the turbot, the tackle and bait used will also catch blonde ray. It is also a ploy of the experienced bank angler to fish a 'flyer' from his 15–20 ft (4·5–6 m) turbot trace. The flyer uses a smaller hook and is baited for plaice, because – although not prolific on these offshore banks – the plaice which are occasionally caught there are real 'stumpers', big 5 lb (2·25 kg) plus fish! So it can be an interesting and yet relaxing day's fishing.

Turbot can also be caught from the sand scour, which is scoured out on the tidal side of wrecks lying on a sandy bottom. Most times if the truth be known, wreck-caught turbot are accidentally caught by anglers wreck fishing for other species. Either the skipper's anchoring is a little short or the anglers sinker is too light or too heavy and the bait ends up in the scour. Which is not actually such a bad place for it to end up: deliberately fishing the scour (which can often be distinctly seen on your echo sounder) can provide an interesting day's fishing.

Tackle

Downtide, conventional tackle is best kept in the middle 20–30 lb (9–13·5 kg) class bracket, because turbot and blonde ray grow to 30 lb (13·5 kg) plus. Both are experts at 'kiting' in the tide in order to exert maximum pressure on your tackle. Boat rods from Shimano, Daiwa, Shakespeare etc, are all well up to the task as are their mid-range boat reels.

Uptide fishing is a superb method of catching these fish. The heavy tides and potential weight

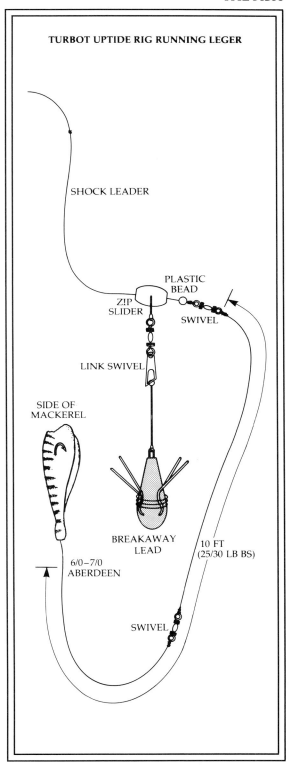

TURBOT UPTIDE RIG RUNNING LEGER

SHOCK LEADER

PLASTIC BEAD

ZIP SLIDER

SWIVEL

LINK SWIVEL

SIDE OF MACKEREL

BREAKAWAY LEAD

10 FT (25/30 LB BS)

6/0–7/0 ABERDEEN

SWIVEL

Peter Peck, Chairman of the English section of the European Federation of Sea Anglers holds aloft a fine turbot, caught from the sandbanks a mile or so off Salcombe. Bait was a whole side of mackerel fished on a long trace.

of the fish dictate the use of the heaviest of uptide outfits.

Method

Fishing downtide, use a conventional medium weight running ledger, and a zip slider carrying a heavy watch lead. The slider is stopped by bead and swivel, with from the swivel a 15–20 ft (4·5–6 m) trace and one, sometimes two, swivels, one of which is a three-way swivel to carry a 'flyer' for plaice, or even to carry another turbot bait.

If you are fishing a sandbank, search the area thoroughly with your sounder and note the position of the sandbank's crest on your Decca as you motor uptide to anchor. Drop the anchor well uptide and let your boat back on its warp until your echo sounder shows that you are about halfway up the sandbank. The objective of the exercise is to get your bait just over the top of the bank below, so that your bait fishes just over the top on the leeward side of the sandbank's crest.

Uptide casting places a restraint on the length of trace which can be used. However, with a slow, gentle lob to take your sinker 20 yd (18 m) instead of 40, a ten ft (3 m) trace can be employed and has proven to be adequate when used with a zip slider and running ledger. When uptiding, you can position your boat right on the sandbank's crest and cast your bait in relationship to it. I am sure that in these circumstances the uptide advantage is not so much in the method, but in the ability to position your bait accurately every time.

Best baits

There is some conflict of opinion amongst anglers who fish regularly for turbot, some say live sandeel is the best bait and others swear by a whole side of fresh mackerel. Then there are those like me who fish a side of mackerel on the end hook and a live sandeel on the flyer. I have heard and read that turbot take crab, razorfish, squid etc, but all the turbot I have ever seen caught on rod and line have come to fish baits.

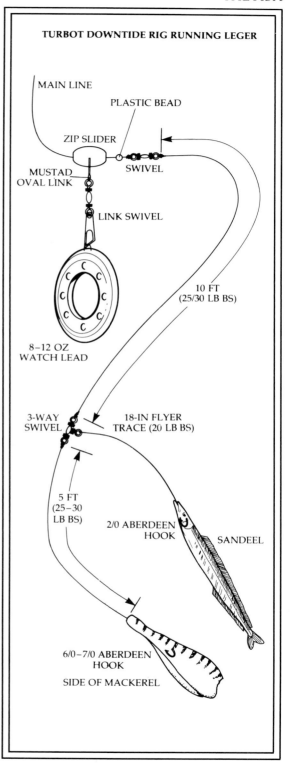

TURBOT DOWNTIDE RIG RUNNING LEGER

MAIN LINE

PLASTIC BEAD

ZIP SLIDER

SWIVEL

MUSTAD OVAL LINK

LINK SWIVEL

10 FT (25/30 LB BS)

8–12 OZ WATCH LEAD

3-WAY SWIVEL

18-IN FLYER TRACE (20 LB BS)

5 FT (25–30 LB BS)

2/0 ABERDEEN HOOK

SANDEEL

6/0–7/0 ABERDEEN HOOK

SIDE OF MACKEREL

Hooks

The heavier 6/0 and 7/0 Mustad Aberdeens are my favourites, with similar size uptide hooks and Kamasan close behind. Some anglers prefer the strength of heavier hook patterns such as the O'Shaughnessey, but I have never found the need.

Trace line for turbot should be slightly heavier than you might normally use, 30 lb (13·5 kg) is standard. If you make your traces up few days before, wind them onto boards, avoid putting the line back on spools. This way the traces are far less likely to tangle. When a turbot picks up your bait it is often just a tic of the rod tip, the second knock is much harder and thats when you should strike. Often fish are missed because anglers do not detect the first nibble and wait too long after the second knock and the fish spits the bait out and goes to find something else to eat. Avoid gaffing turbot if you can; a very large landing net is standard equipment. Watch out for the second turbot which will often accompany the hooked fish to the surface.

WHITING

Whiting are not a hard fighting sport fish, but they taste good and are fun to catch. If I am going for whiting I like to take a couple of cool boxes and several ice packs for each box. I clean and wash each fish as soon as it is caught and put it straight into the cool box. This way the whiting are ready for the freezer as soon as you get home.

Tackle

A general-purpose 20 or 30 lb (9 or 13·5 kg) class outfit with a standard multiplier is perfectly adequate for whiting. If you decide to go after specimen whiting, then use a 12 lb (5·5 kg) class outfit with a single hook and 24 in (60 cm) trace, rigged as for a flying collar.

Method

It is not unusual to employ two or three hooks for whiting paternostered off your main line,

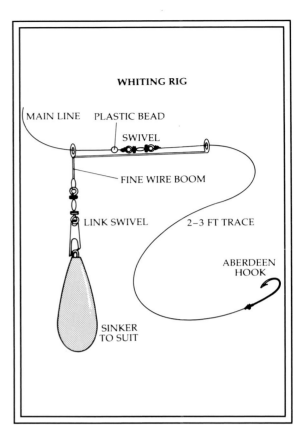

using booms such as the hookless type, or simple three way swivel paternosters. There is no need for long snood lengths off each paternoster, 8–10 in (20–25 cm) of line to the hook is enough.

Use a sinker heavy enough to hold bottom. Find the fish on your echo sounder, anchor or drift the Decca co-ordinates, depending on the tidal strength. The bites will be positive and unmistakable.

Many anglers simply use their mackerel feathers, sweetening each hook with a worm or small mackerel strip: don't knock it, they catch a lot of whiting.

Best bait

Ragworm, lugworm, small mackerel strips, side of sandeel, etc. Whiting when they are on the feed, are not too fussy about the bait you are using!

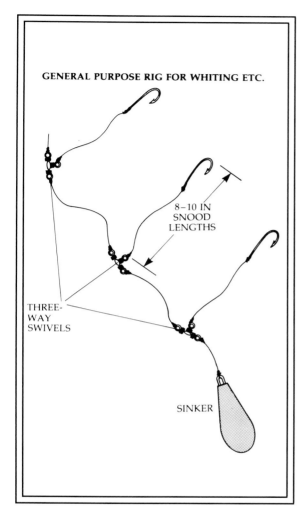

GENERAL PURPOSE RIG FOR WHITING ETC.

8–10 IN SNOOD LENGTHS

THREE-WAY SWIVELS

SINKER

Hooks

Fine wire Aberdeens or virtually any reasonably long shanked hook. The long shank serves no other purpose than to make unhooking easier. Sizes 1/0 to 4/0.

WRASSE

The ballan wrasse is a rock- and weed-dwelling species. It is another of those species which anglers pursue more for sport than for the table. A good wrasse will weigh in at about 5 lbs (2·25 kg) or slightly more, although my diver friends tell me they have seen the occasional fish into double figures around the offshore reefs. The present record nine-pounder was caught by charter skipper Mike Goodacre on live sandeel on the Eddystone Reef, so if you want your name in the record book the wrasse is a good target. The inshore boat angler has the advantage of being able to pursue such lesser known species as wrasse over isolated and little known rock marks.

Tackle

The ballan wrasse is a tough little fighter which will take you into the bottom in an instant. So the gear has to be able to apply some real pressure to keep the fish's head up and out of the bottom. A light uptide casting rod 3–5 oz (85–140 gm) casting weight, about 9 ft (2·7 m) long is ideal. Your standard boatcasting reel loaded with 15–18 lb (6·5–8 kg) line will be adequate in most circumstances, but if you find some big ballans, then you might well have to uprate to 25 lb (11 kg) line.

End rigs for wrasse should be kept simple yet strong; a simple ledger with the sinker fastened with a weak link of say 10 lb (4·5 kg) line, so that if the sinker becomes caught in the bottom it can be broken out without losing much gear. This weak link is known as a 'Rotten Bottom'.

Float fishing for wrasse, especially over the inaccessible and dangerous rocks which large wrasse survive so well in, is really the only technique which has any chance of success. I still use my uptide rod but change the reel for a hefty fixed spool with a fast retrieve and firm but smooth clutch. If the wrasse wants to take line, then it will have to work hard for every inch!

Method

Often the shore angler will have a favourite reef or rock which large wrasse are known to inhabit, but the shore angler can only fish one side of it. When the boat angler comes along, drops anchor and begins to catch fish from the seaward side, that is the moment when the shore angler gives serious consideration to getting a boat! It is also likely that there will be

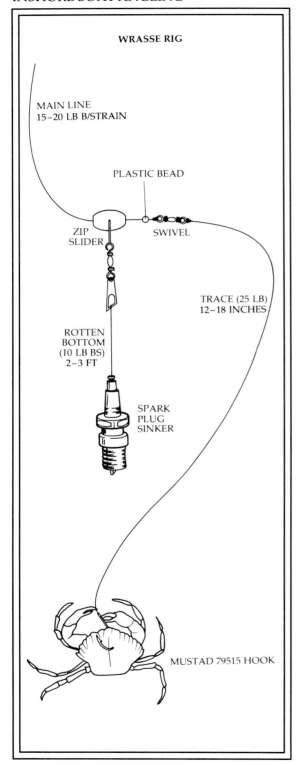

WRASSE RIG

MAIN LINE
15–20 LB B/STRAIN

PLASTIC BEAD

ZIP
SLIDER

SWIVEL

TRACE (25 LB)
12–18 INCHES

ROTTEN
BOTTOM
(10 LB BS)
2–3 FT

SPARK
PLUG
SINKER

MUSTAD 79515 HOOK

lumps of rock extending way out of range of the shore angler. By searching the ground with your echo sounder, unsuspected, often unknown spurs of rock can be discovered. If they come near the surface they will be on your chart, so look carefully and proceed with caution this close in.

A simple ledger fixed or running with the sinker held by a rotten bottom is the bottom fishing method. If your sounder shows a good depth of weed this rotten bottom can be several feet long to hold your baited hook just clear of the weed, making the fish come out of cover for the bait. The sinker can be an old nut or bolt, a favourite is an old spark plug. If you use spark plugs boil them first, clean any oil residue from them which could put the fish off.

The float fishing rig is a standard sliding float rig, but using a big float. My floats for wrasse fishing are a foot (0·3 m) long by an inch (2·5 cm) in diameter, carrying about 1½ oz (40 gm) of lead. When a big wrasse takes your bait, the bite is very positive and even a big float like this will go well under.

Baits

For big wrasse there is but one bait, a hard back crab about 1½ in (3–4 cm) across the back. Don't use any crabs less than an inch across or you will be plagued by small wrasse. Peeler crabs also work well but I prefer to use peelers for other species, they are not necessary for wrasse. Prawns are a wrasse delicacy, but the smallest of wrasse can manage the largest prawn for a snack. I sometimes use prawn bait if I think there is a chance of a bass over the same ground. King ragworm is best used as an early season bait, at other times of year it will attract legions of tiny wrasse, which will strip the worm from the hook in seconds.

Hooks

Hooks need to be strong yet sharp and the best wrasse hook I have found is the Mustad 79515. The Real Tackle uptide hooks come a close second. Sizes 1/0, 2/0 and 3/0 are ideal, the actual size depending on the size of bait used.

If you cannot jump the hook free over the side of the boat, net the wrasse inboard and wrap it in a sopping wet towel. Hold the fish still, remove the hook and return the wrasse to the water as quickly and as gently as possible.

ANSWER TO THE NAVIGATIONAL PROBLEM ON P 67

The decisions you would arrive at in this situation, if your Decca gives out, would to a large degree depend on how well you were prepared for such an eventuality. You will see at once the necessity of taking your charts and navigational gear with you, even if it does seem to be a nuisance. So what do you do?

First, keep on course but slow the boat down and get your chart out. Draw a line between the Coalboat position and the West Rutts Reef, if you then make an educated guess at your position on this line, taking into account how long you have been travelling, you should have a reasonable indication of your position. From this position, using your Bretton Plotter take a bearing on the Tinker buoy, a West Cardinal buoy guarding the eastern entrance to Plymouth Sound. Steer this course at a reduced speed, say five knots. How do you know that you are making five knots? Very simply, because you will have prepared for this situation by marking a throttle setting using your Decca's speed over ground facility – when it was working properly! Scaling off the chart with your plotter, the distance from your starting point to the Tinker Buoy is approximately six and a half miles, so it should take you around an hour and twenty minutes to come up to the Tinker. Now the Tinker Buoy is a West Cardinal Mark, which tells you that the hazard which it guards lies to the east of the Buoy; this is unlikely to bother us too much in our little boat, but too far to the east could put us on the rocks. So after an hour or so you are watching and listening, sounding off with the Foghorn every now and again to let others know that you are about. With luck you will come upon the Tinker, or one of the other buoys which are in its vicinity which will give you an accurate fix on your position. Assuming, however, you cannot find a buoy after the hour-and-twenty-minute run, you then look to the Echo sounder to indicate whether the ground beneath the keel has turned to rock; even if you have missed the buoys, you should find the Tinker Shoal; sure enough, the sounder shows rock rising to nearly twenty feet beneath the boat. Your knowledge of the state of the tide tells you that you have found the high point of the rock. This gives a pretty good indication of position, now there is a choice . . . do you head for the east end or the west end of the breakwater? My choice on this hypothetical day would be to go for the west end; the reason for my choice is the fact that the lighthouse on the west end sounds a mournful old bell in foggy conditions, and this sound will tell me how close I am to the breakwater. Turning to a course of 325 degrees and scaling the distance off at one mile, you know that after 10 minutes or so at five knots you should be up to the breakwater. After 12 minutes, the bell is deafening you and the breakwater lighthouse looms out of the mist.

From there on in it is easy, you know what course to steer, you have done it before and the course is logged in your little black book. But without your charts, you could have been another lifeboat statistic . . . the sea has no favourites!

Laurie Jackson feathering for mackerel aboard his own boat en route to a wreck fishing session. The Well Away *is a 22-ft diesel-driven Seaworker.*

INDEX

Page numbers in *italic* refer to illustrations